HEALED
By His
Promise

One Family's Journey from
Impossible to Glorious

STEPHANIE WALLS & REMINGTON WALLS

Printed in the United States of America

First Printing, 2024

ISBN 13: 979-8-9886776-7-3

Disclaimer: This book is intended solely as a source of spiritual guidance and inspiration. The contents of this book are not, and should not be construed as, medical advice. We encourage readers to seek professional diagnosis, treatments, and advice from qualified health professionals for any medical conditions. The practices discussed in the book are meant to complement, not replace, any medical or therapeutic treatments.

A note about the Bible versions: Bible verses are pulled from Stephanie's favorite version, NIV (New International Version), Remington's favorite version, NKJV (New King James Version), and in a couple places, the NSAB (New American Standard Bible), because we feel the NASB is the most literal translation.

Dedication

To Andrew Wommack, Gary and Drenda Keesee, I am eternally grateful to the truths you shared that changed my life. To Mom and Dad for creating a home that served the Lord. To my beautiful wife Jessica for being someone to walk with and grow in the Lord together. Above all else, thank you Jesus for the price you paid for my, and everyone else's, freedom.

—Remington Walls

A special thanks to Don and Sandy who had the courage and boldness to step out in faith and teach me the truth about healing. To the seeds sown by the late John Osteen's teachings and the teachings of Andrew Wommack and Gary Kessee. To Donna, thank you for a lifelong journey of friendship. To my husband, Mike, and sons, Dalton, and Remington, I've been blessed by your love! To my awesome and powerful Jesus, thank you for Your sacrifice! Your life changes *EVERYTHING*!

—Stephanie Walls

Contents

Introduction

Have you ever witnessed a miracle? Something that no one thought would change or work out, yet you saw, firsthand, the power of God? That was our family, with a story that even we were stunned by until we realized the amazing power God can bring to someone's life, if they trust and believe that He only wants good for us, His precious children.

Sometimes, we don't even realize that there is a reason to hope for a miracle because we never imagined one existed. Our brains focus too much on the right now and not enough on the much bigger things happening with God's hand.

Our family has dealt with a life sentence disease that changed everything about how we operated together. We've also faced the terrifying diagnosis of cancer and what that would mean for our future. As we worried and fretted, we had an *aha* moment where we realized…

What if we are looking at this all wrong? What if God didn't operate the way we thought He did?

What if there was more to our relationship with God than we realized?

Those thoughts led us to delve deep into our faith and to ask hundreds of difficult questions that, ultimately, not only brought both of us closer to God, but to each other and to the rest of our family.

It also brought us not one, but two miraculous healings that you'll have to read about to believe. We wrote this book because we wanted to show you the lessons we learned, the profound impact they had on our lives, and to give you a roadmap of scripture-based suggestions for doing the same.

These lessons have been forged by both trials and triumphs of experience. We sincerely hope they'll be a beacon for your path, too. And a sign that what He has done for our family, He has also *already done for you.*

—Stephanie and Remington Walls

"So then faith comes by hearing,
and hearing by the Word of God."
Romans 10:17 (NKJV)

Chapter 1

The Principle of Mercy

Remington

Do you believe your entire life can change in one encounter with the Lord? That one moment, one discovery, and one conversation with God can transform every part of your existence?

Frankly, I didn't believe that. I was dealing with a diagnosis that had a huge impact on every aspect of my life and I was struggling—deeply struggling—in my relationship with God.

Drifting away from the faith of my childhood as I got older, I knew that there was more. Some answer that I was missing. Of course, there was, and my life was changed forever by the incorruptible seed and amazing power of the Word of God. Just not before I went through hell and back.

When I was a kid, I was diagnosed with a lifelong disease. For the first couple years of my life, whenever I ingested any food or drink, I screamed in agony and cried in pain while choking and gagging to get it down. My parents, not knowing what the issue was or how to help me, frantically took me from doctor to specialist, who ran dozens of tests. It took years for them to get any definitive answers.

When I was three, my parents finally found a gastroenterologist specializing in eating disorders, who did a series of bloodwork and tests on me. These test results revealed a high white blood cell count called eosinophils—the kind of blood cells that become active when you have certain allergic reactions, diseases, or infections—and that concerned him, so he scheduled an upper endoscopy.

The results of that test launched a series of events that changed our family forever. We finally had a diagnosis, but it was a grim one for me. I had Eosinophilic Esophagitis, also known as EoE, an inflammation of the esophagus (the tube connecting the mouth to the stomach).

Meaning, I was unable to pass any solid food without it deteriorating my esophagus.

My parents and doctor wanted to focus on treatment immediately because the more they attempted to feed me at home, the weaker I got. I just couldn't keep the food down. Essentially, the thing that sustains life for most people caused too much damage to my esophageal tissue and thus, my body.

I don't remember those first appointments, but I can imagine the panic and worry my parents felt once they realized I literally couldn't eat food. Ever. What a life-changing thing for any child, any person, to endure.

We eventually made our way to another specialized clinic in Ohio that could potentially treat me. After booking a flight and arriving at a family member's home in Columbus, we made the two-hour drive south to Cincinnati.

Over the years, we made so many trips to Ohio for tests and endoscopies that I lost count.

The travel wasn't fun. In fact, it was dreadful. We got to spend some time together as a family, which was nice. However, while most kids were traveling for holiday vacation or on summer break to the beach, I was flying back and forth from my family's house to the hospital to check my esophagus via pictures from an endoscopy, plus my eosinophil count through a biopsy, to confirm that I was still sick.

I had a strong hope that I would improve and be able to live a normal life when we started treatment after my very first appointment, but it didn't take long to feel looming discouragement instead. Every trip meant an endoscopy, and every endoscopy still showed a high eosinophil count, and that meant failure. They'd try me on different foods, but we always went right back to square one. I had an answer, but still no hope for healing.

The only sliver of joy during these trips would eventually be our tradition of ordering dinner in, when I got a little older and after my esophagus had healed some. This was always pizza. I inhaled as many pieces as I could and it was delicious, despite all of the physical consequences.

Those didn't matter because it felt like my soul was revived when I was sitting at the table, eating with my family, and living some semblance of what I imagined a normal life to be. It also served as a glimpse to a day in the life of a fully-healed me, which was both hopeful and hope-breaking.

Every time I went to the hospital, the results were worse. It had been confirmed at that initial appointment that my esophagus was so severely damaged that I would have to replace *all* food and drink with a substitute formula to promote its healing.

All? Every single food and drink? I didn't fully understand what the doctors were saying, or the weight those words held. Especially when, that same night, my parents took me out to dinner and said, "Order whatever you want."

At the age of four, my life was suddenly simplified to a single meal option. I didn't understand that yet; all I saw was this food free-for-all. What I couldn't have guessed was that this was my parents' way of preparing me for a last supper of sorts.

As the waiter brought my food out, both my mom and dad explained to me that this would be my last full meal for a very long time. From then on, I would have to drink a "special" drink instead so my body could heal itself. They were referring to elemental formula which would be part of my life for the next nineteen years.

Elemental formula is a liquid, similar to the consistency of what they give to infants and is prescribed to EoE patients because it's much easier for the body to break down than solid food. The amino acid formula would replace every slice of pizza, bite of steak, and french fry I was used to having for the foreseeable future.

As we moved into this new way of eating, it was hard for me to understand that I couldn't eat food anymore, especially when the whole world and everything the world does seemed to revolve around it. Birthday parties, holiday dinners, even a simple meal became a painful reminder of what I was missing.

My parents taught me to focus on the blessings in my life, like the fact that I had the formula as an option to sustain me and help me remain positive while so many others were in pain, but it was hard to see that some days.

The bodies of the rarest sufferers of this disease—which my mom spent hours, if not days, researching—are affected to the point where they can't eat *any* food whatsoever. This was the diagnosis I received. It immediately made me a sort of outcast in the world because I was never going to go grab a burger with my friends or get an ice cream in the summertime.

That one difference between me and other kids my age put me out on an island of embarrassment and shame, leaving me feeling isolated while I was learning to adjust to the disease.

Any sense of belonging was just out of reach, and I always questioned the reasoning behind a loving God who let my family, or me, go through this and for allowing this to happen. I just couldn't understand why He would subject me to such a trial in the first place. This is the way we thought growing up because it was what religion taught us. We didn't know any better at the time.

As my esophagus began to recover because I was consuming exclusively elemental formula, my doctor gave us approval to start food trials at home. Every few months, we'd try something and I'd have to eat a certain amount of food (with a single ingredient) for a specific period of time. If I developed any symptoms such as pain in my esophagus, coughing, or vomiting, the doctor said I had to immediately halt the trial and undergo a recovery period (which would usually last about the length of time I'd tried the food for, plus a couple of weeks) before starting the next one.

When I had the rare successful trial and I'd experienced no tangible symptoms, it was always followed by a trip to Ohio and another endoscopy. Every single time, it showed under-surface results of still having that same, high eosinophil count or a damaged, deteriorating esophagus.

To put that damage into context, when a doctor shines their flashlight into the back of your mouth, the lining of the entire esophagus should be smooth, like the start of your throat. Mine looked like a clenched fist. Rigid with many grooves, which was another sign of a failed food trial.

The rug was repeatedly pulled out from under me. A strong feeling of despair and sense of hopelessness always followed this disappointment because food trials were my last hope of getting better and feeling normal, and they were not working out.

This went on for years and with every trial that failed, my hope of eating normally continued to disappear. It seemed as if nothing was working or would ever work for me—like my life was destined to be this way, and nothing would ever change. My hopes would be repeatedly dashed all over when each new food started to work against me, damaging my esophagus again.

My primary go-to to relieve this stress and to mentally escape from my situation quickly became sports. It provided a sense of normalcy that I craved.

On the field, I could belong and feel almost like everyone else, but I realized I had to be selective about the sports I played. Burning a lot of calories while not being able to put more in via solid food was a recipe for a dangerous amount of weight loss, and I was already pretty skinny.

The longer this give-and-take took to balance my desire to play with my body's need for sustenance, the more I felt anger and frustration simmering inside me. I remember crying out to God multiple times, asking Him, "Why me?"

There was never an answer. Night after night I begged Him to heal my body and, again, I heard no answers. Every single time I opened one of those shakes (I consumed up to twenty a day), I heard that silence from God.

Then I'd go to my parents to ask them why this happened. Their response was always along the lines of, "I don't know why, but God knew you and our family were strong enough to handle this."

That response rattled my faith. Why would anyone want to devote themselves to a God like that? A God who gave you a disease simply because He decided you were stronger than the next person and could tolerate it? I started to view God as a harsh, mean Power who was devoid of love.

I couldn't have been further from the truth.

When my mom and I wrote our first book several years ago, *Home Plate: A True Story of Resilience,* we didn't understand at the time what God's promises were or what they meant for our healing. We didn't understand what His foundational truths are, including that of His unconditional love and His promises to us as His children.

As I asked more questions and had more doubts, I didn't realize God was continually trying to pull me closer to Him in a pure display of mercy and love. Not out of punishment or out of an impossible burden. He wanted a relationship with me, and to share His nature with me—but I just kept getting further from the Father with every next step I took.

Stephanie

Fellow parents will understand the indescribable pain of witnessing your child in distress—a heartache our Almighty Father knows all too well. The minute I became a mother, I understood God's unconditional love for us. However, I struggled to find a greater purpose in my child's suffering. How could I see the good in that?

That was a question I asked every time I watched Remington, my youngest son, struggle to eat. When he was born, he'd get sick and vomit after a bottle, no matter which formula we tried. We hoped solids would make a difference but when we began introducing foods into his diet, he still kept getting sick. Then he started choking while trying to swallow whatever we gave him.

Nothing I did—rocking him, setting him on top of the dryer, singing to him—could relax my sweet boy. It was heartbreaking. In those early days I often felt helpless, and the situation was hopeless.

Getting sick and vomiting over and over again was tremendously harsh on Remington's young body. It kept him from gaining weight as a growing boy should. Our doctors prescribed him nebulizers and steroids while telling us to continue his normal diet, all to no avail. My husband, Mike, and I were growing deeply concerned, becoming sleep-deprived like our two sons, and at a total loss for how to ease Remington's pain.

I became desperate to find the solution. I wanted a remedy that would heal him and, in the process, bring our family back from the brink of dysfunction. An ill child, particularly a sick infant, puts a tremendous strain on any family, and Remington's health became our sole focus, invariably taking our attention away from other areas. We struggled, as many families do, to balance it all.

I would pray for God to give us answers, while I was also thanking Him for giving my family this burden as a way to show others His light. That prayer was my very first mistake, and such a prideful thing to say, but I didn't know that yet. All we wanted to do was to fix him.

I can only tell you that my intentions were good, and that I thought my faith was strong.

Finally, when Remington was three years old and after already seeing multiple doctors, we took him to see a gastroenterologist. That doctor told us our son had Eosinophilic Esophagitis, or EoE. This is an inflammatory condition where the esophagus becomes filled with eosinophils, a type of white blood cell that causes inflammation when present in high amounts. That inflammation stiffens the esophagus to the point where solid food can't pass to the stomach.

This was the explanation we needed for Remington's symptoms! For a moment, we were relieved, but then we asked what this meant for his future. We spoke of the "what-ifs" and the worst-case scenarios while also trying to predict what we would do when that possible worst happened.

All I heard was that my son would never, ever be able to keep any food down or eat like everyone else does. I kept imagining the heartache and difficulties that lay ahead for him and saw a dimly-lit, maybe even dark, road. Those were fears which I now know should never be spoken aloud because, whether positive or negative, those words hold power, a concept that took me a long time to understand.

The doctor suggested we begin an elimination diet to narrow down his food choices, but his problems persisted. Soon, Remington had hollow, dark circles under his eyes, almost like a raccoon, and he cried quite a bit, never really smiling. It was sad to see him trying so hard to be present and able in life, but nearly wasting away in front of us with every extra calorie he spent.

Once he was removed from all foods, mealtime was a challenge and we struggled with how to include Remington yet not remind him of all he missed out on. That led us to adopt household habits that had good intentions, but unfortunately had a negative impact on our children. To avoid Remington being tempted by the smell of our food, Mike and I decided to eat separately. We took turns, each one dining in our bedroom with Dalton, our eldest son.

That isolation, confusion, and stress were felt by everyone in our home. Despite doing our best to provide our support to both children, we disrupted the very sense of stability and routine children thrive on, especially that of family mealtimes.

Then Mike and I went to a marriage conference led by Gary Chapman. He suggested we stop focusing on Remington's disease and focus on conversation at the table, instead. Not the food.

We realized that by isolating ourselves when we ate, we were teaching our son we would alter our lives for him and needed to teach him how to adapt to a foodless world in order to thrive. It was difficult for me to manage that stress as a mother and partner in the head of the household. I leaned on prayer as much as I could.

When we returned to the gastroenterologist a year later, Remington was four and preparing for another endoscopy to see if the eosinophils had lessened. We were disappointed to find out that the EoE had spread to his lower esophagus. Learning that his condition had not only failed to improve but had actually worsened and spread, left us frustrated and worried for the future.

Mike and I were fearful about what this prognosis would mean for our little boy's life as he moved forward and did things like go to school, play sports, and go to college. I found myself battling anger towards God, feeling as though He was permitting this to happen. My prayers up until then had been constant pleas for our son's health and his life, but now I questioned why I should persist in prayer when it seemed that every request went unheard.

I was blinded by my focus on the problem. I didn't know it then, but I should have been praying for the result and standing firm in faith.

Standing firm in faith, to me, is agreeing that God's will means total health, and I believe it is true. I agree with and lean, or stand, on the scriptures in His Word.

That sounds odd, I know, but it's true, and in this book I'll talk about how that shift in my thinking and in my relationship with God transformed my own health and, later, Remington's too.

For many years, I focused on the kind of self-centered prayer that would give me an immediate solution or a "sign" of what to do next. I didn't realize there was so much more to using scripture for answers and the power that God could have in my life.

Mark 11:22-24 (NIV) says, "Have faith in God," Jesus answered. "Truly I tell you, if anyone says to this mountain, 'Go, throw yourself into the sea,' and does not doubt in their heart but believes that what they say will happen, it will be done for them. Therefore I tell you, whatever you ask for in prayer, believe that you have received it, and it will be yours."

The "mountain" to me was the symbol of everything our family was going through. Changing or resolving Remington's EoE diagnosis felt as impossible as moving a mountain. How could any of this ever be healed?

I read this verse from Mark countless times, not understanding that the verse was saying that we can *command* the mountain to leave, and if we truly believe in the power of our faith-filled words, then it will come to pass. The mountain *will* move. I wasn't ready to see or understand that yet.

So no, nothing changed overnight when it came to treating Remington. After receiving that devastating diagnosis when he was three, nothing changed for years. We were constantly in and out of hospitals and doctor's offices.

Each time we traveled back to Cincinnati Children's for yet another biopsy, we were told that his esophagus still showed signs of eosinophilia. While this was tough to hear and accept, we couldn't deny that Rem's body had begun to show signs of healing once he eliminated all food and began drinking the formula. The dark circles began to lessen, and he began to laugh and smile again.

Even so, the worry and want never left us. My husband and I passionately sought complete healing for him through prayer and maintained our commitment to regular church attendance, but our family did not experience the total restoration we yearned for.

We felt abandoned by God.

In the stillness of night when I cuddled Remington to sleep, I would gently tell him that he had been "chosen" by God to shoulder this hardship. I explained to him that our experience was meant to show others the power of God's love and light. That maybe other people would see our family's perseverance in our struggles and be inspired to do the same for whatever they were going through. I suggested that God must have believed we possessed the strength to navigate this journey.

When I told Remington about this strength and explained how God had chosen us for this task, I was mistaken in that belief.

Pride, in its most destructive form, is elevating yourself above others with a self-righteous attitude, even above God. In my arrogance, I had placed myself above the Lord and wrongfully accused Him of "choosing" us.

At that point in my spiritual journey, my grasp of God's promises was still rudimentary. I understood the principles of prayer and faith but only at a basic level. In retrospect, I was still finding my feet in this faith journey. Both my husband and I look back and see that we were at the early stages of our Christian walk, like spiritual infants or baby Christians.

I've often heard ministers tell the story of the book of Job, as I'm sure many people have, where it's suggested that God burdens us with trials to make us stronger. Another common theme I've heard from Job's story refers to when he says, "The Lord gave and the Lord has taken away," after sitting atop a hill with nothing left to his name. Many use this to explain why terrible things happen to good people (and it is what I thought that story meant, too), but this is not what Job's story teaches. A careful reading of Job's story paints a different picture.

Note that what happened to Job is explained in the Old Covenant (which is the law people lived under; the Old Testament is what is commonly known as the books of the Bible from that time period), when sacrifices were made to the Lord prior to Jesus' sacrifice on the cross. Under the New Covenant, which was created by the act of Jesus hanging on the cross for us, our slates have been cleaned and our debts (sins) have been paid. The Old Covenant was meant to lead us to Christ by pointing to our need of a Savior. The New Covenant *is* Christ, and now *He* is the way. (Hebrews 6:13 NIV)

In Job 3:4-5, Job's children spoke ill of God and led sinful lives, indulging in frivolous pleasures without repentance. It was Job himself who made burnt offerings (sacrifices) on their behalf. When Job went to God and voiced his fears about his life—that his children would curse Him and as a result he would lose everything—this worry ultimately materialized for him. All his children perished due to their wickedness and sin.

It was only when the Lord reproached Job, questioning his understanding, that Job acknowledged his errored thinking. Job 3:25-26 (NIV) states, "What I feared has come upon me; what I dreaded has happened to me. I have no peace, no quietness; I have no rest, but only turmoil."

The Bible tells us that our words hold power, and sadly, Job's fears came true because he gave them voice. That was the pivotal realization for me—I was giving voice to my fears and unwittingly making them come true. It would be several years and yet another medical trial for our family before this lesson fully took root inside me.

Job 38:2 (NIV) is the verse that shows the Lord's challenge to Job (and to those of us who speak the worst outcomes into reality): "Who is this that obscures my plans with words without knowledge?"

God is being quite stern because Job is not relying on His promises of life and prosperity.

A few verses later, in Job 42 (NIV), is Job's humble response to the Lord: "I know that you can do all things; no purpose of yours can be thwarted. You asked, 'Who is this that obscures my plans without knowledge?' Surely I spoke of things I did not understand, things too wonderful for me to know. You said, 'Listen now, and I will speak; I will question you, and you shall answer me.' My ears had heard of you but now my eyes have seen you. Therefore I despise myself and repent in dust and ashes."

Many people are incorrectly taught that God inflicts suffering upon us to teach us a lesson, but that is not true at all.

My belief that God intentionally burdened us with these trials to shine His light upon others suggested He deliberately withheld Remington's healing all this time, but God does not hold back anything from us. It is our own *absence* of knowledge, as Job pointed out, that keeps us in darkness. Hosea 4:6 (NIV) powerfully attests to this fact, "My people are destroyed for their lack of knowledge."

There's so much more to being a Christian than just being saved from an eternity of hell. Salvation is only the beginning. It is the first and most important step, but there are many other promises of the Kingdom that we are heirs to as His children! There are many other blessings, fruits we can experience, after we take that first step.

I think because many of us don't know how to tap into the "fruits" of God's Kingdom here on Earth, we become resentful because we are still struggling to make it through the day, like I was. I was grateful I would go to Heaven when I died, but that seemed so far off from my own reality while living in the now. It certainly didn't seem to resolve the pain my son was enduring.

Becoming a mother helped me to think of God as my own father, mildly shaking his head at my missteps, yet always gracing me with a warm smile and radiating His love for me—patiently waiting for me to align with His path. I did the same with my own children and saw the change in their lives when they finally found their footing.

For me, it took some time to align with God and what He wants (and already provides) for us, but once I did, I saw that the remedy to healing Remington was in front of us all along. We just had to reach out and receive it!

Chapter 2

The Principle of Love

Remington

When I was a kid, I heard people say "what you don't know won't hurt you" a thousand times. As a teenager, it was annoying, but as I became an adult, I realized I disagreed with this saying. What I didn't know about God and about my faith was precisely what was hurting me.

Hosea 4:6 (NIV) says, "My people are destroyed for lack of knowledge," and it was an echo of my spiritual walk as a young person.

For a long time, I held onto the belief that God chooses who He heals and maybe, for whatever reason, He hadn't chosen to heal me. I didn't know why it was happening, just that this was the hand of cards I was dealt. I had no idea that my lack of knowing what God wants for me was actually the answer to *why*.

I grew up with the same group of friends and classmates from kindergarten all throughout high school, so everyone around me knew my story, or at least had heard of it. I was just so numb to it, so used to it, I wasn't even bothered when people asked me questions.

Despite my willingness to talk about what made me different, at the same time I was like many kids, trying to be accepted by my peers and find my own unique niche. Whether I was looking to be the most popular, the most valuable player on the baseball team, or doing things like staying out late and talking to the most popular girls, skipping class, ignoring homework or being the class clown—I tried on every literal and metaphorical t-shirt just trying to fit in.

Unbeknownst to me, I was yielding more and more to the darkness and drifting further and further from the light. I'd relegated God to the sidelines of my life. Then another challenge came to our family's doorstep and rattled us.

In 2017, my mom went in for a routine mammogram that showed a lump on her scan. Mom was the rock of our family, the one all of us turned to when we were scared or uncertain, and the thought of a cancer diagnosis taking her from us was not easy. It made me face another type of reality and the very real possibility of losing her.

I thought about her undergoing chemotherapy, radiation therapy, the surgical removal of the cancer, and the reconstructive surgery afterward. The list of potential options and treatments only grew longer, and each one seemed to come with its own set of risks and side effects. I could see my mom was overwhelmed, but she still displayed a sense of calm and continued to amaze me by how she handled the news.

Our relationship and her attitude had always been full of love and optimism and her faith has always been strong, especially as I struggled to understand my own diagnosis and relationship with God. Though she hadn't yet discovered the promises that changed everything for our family, she stood strong in her belief of the outcome and knew she would be okay.

I knew she was a warrior and had no doubt she would pull through this because of her time-tested strength and courage. I also didn't worry as much because I was a junior in high school, focused on all the things kids that age typically are. I didn't think about the Lord, live for the Lord, or (quite honestly) care about the Lord. I was looking for comfort in the things that typical teenage boys run to: girls, parties, and sports, especially baseball. The only thoughts I had about church and religion were that, at some point, I hoped I'd go to Heaven. I didn't really get any deeper than that.

My mom, however, after meeting with her childhood friend, Donna, and Donna's parents, was introduced to new teachings on scripture. These were different than what we'd been taught (or not taught) by religion, and she firmly believed in God's will for her to be fully healed.

She tried to tell me what she was learning many times, but it fell on deaf ears. While I believed that she would be able to experience complete health, when she told me it was God's will for me to be healed, I brushed her off. I couldn't see a future where I was healed.

I had suffered with this disease for my entire life. What would make me believe it would suddenly disappear?

But my mother persisted. While walking around the house singing praise and worship music, saying scripture aloud or reading her Bible, she kept on telling me about the love of God and its transformative power. I couldn't eat a simple sandwich and here she was, talking about transformative power.

Remember, I was a teenager, and those years included a bit of rebellion and looking forward, especially to breaking free of my parents. I was much more interested in experiencing high school and going off to college than listening to her talk about a growing confidence in God's ability to heal.

I'd say things like "You're such a nun," or "Stop with this crap."

I'm not proud of speaking like that to her, but I felt justified in my irritation and insistence on blocking out her words at the time. I thought all the singing and quoting scripture was just a way to run away from the reality of sickness, but she'd experienced a reality I didn't yet understand. She could see herself free from disease and had experienced the truth of God's character, a new reality, The Prince of Peace.

Now, several years later, I understand the impact of my words and how hurtful they must have been for her to hear. Still, she never wavered.

That's what parents do, isn't it? They'll tell us repeatedly the best way to get somewhere and yet we still choose not to listen. When we finally make it to our destination, maybe we're a bit bumped and bruised, but now, we're fully prepared to open our ears because we realize that our parents were right all along. Just as He promises us in the Word, our Heavenly Father never wavers and is always there, waiting for us to be ready to hear and accept His message (Isaiah 30:18).

I was so hardened by my previous experiences of disappointment and shame that I wasn't hearing that message any more than I'd heard my parents when I was a teenager. I also had a brewing anger within me because I didn't have answers, and just couldn't understand why any of this was happening. I think that was why I got so frustrated with my mom because that was easier than living in this place of unknown, without any answers to hold on to.

My mother never wavered in her love or patience with me, which amazes me to this day. I know not every child is blessed to have parents with such a strong, unconditional love, and that makes me feel doubly grateful for mine. That didn't mean I was ready to jump on the God wagon with her back then, though.

To me, all her suggestions and scriptures were the same messages I had heard for years in church, centered around a set of rules and regulations I had no interest in following. As one of my favorite ministers, Andrew Wommack, said, "If I had told you I was a Christian growing up, I wouldn't have had enough evidence to be convicted of it!"

Going off to college at Valdosta State University became a liberating experience, but it was also a huge learning lesson. My initial reaction was a long sigh of *finally* because I was no longer under my parent's roof and could have what I saw as real fun and do whatever I wanted, when I wanted.

I spent a couple of years as a typical college kid—skipping class, going to parties, meeting girls. Even though I was still empty on the inside, I didn't care. I had a lot of fun with these friends and felt good for a while, until the adrenaline wore off and I was forced to confront those empty feelings again, trying to figure out what would fill the hole in my heart. The more I went to parties and stayed out late, the less the acceptance from my friends and others began to satisfy those deep needs inside me.

I kept pushing the *lack* of feeling down and brushing it off, even making attempts to drown it out with pornography or disguise it with anger, but I eventually got to a point where I couldn't keep ignoring it. None of those distractions could mute the disconnection buried in me, which reared its head in many places, especially church.

I dedicated even less time to going to church and didn't go unless I visited my parents back home for major holidays, like

Easter or Christmas. I'd squirm in the pew the entire sermon, ready for it to end as soon as it started. That was conflicting because I couldn't deny the presence of God in the building on some occasions, and I couldn't figure out why a small part of me left there feeling like I'd *enjoyed* His presence but hadn't enjoyed the feeling of being present in church.

I even found myself being judgmental, questioning why the people sitting around me praised God despite the turmoil that I had been taught was caused by God Himself. I was still angry with God about what I was going through but held onto my belief in Him because I didn't want to go to hell, and I wanted to please my parents by being respectful in church.

My classroom performance began to suffer from skipping so many classes, and so did my chances of earning a spot on the college's baseball team. The coach pulled me aside and made it clear that if I wanted to be part of the team, my size, strength, and speed had to improve. He wasn't singling me out because of the disease at all, but at that point I was only about a hundred and forty pounds and not very strong. I even considered moving back home and attending a community college just so I could play on any team.

College sports are at a much higher level competitively than what I had experienced when I was younger, and that meant a higher bar to meet. I never made an excuse for my performance based on the EoE, because I never wanted to see myself as a victim of disease, and I felt that I was doing right by pushing forward to make the team.

In reality, it was challenging for me to gain weight. I didn't have a lot of knowledge about nutrition or exercise. I also struggled to balance and utilize those two, especially with the elemental formula. Ultimately, my performance didn't meet the standard for the team. Instead of earning a spot to play, I became the team's manager.

To say I was disappointed would be an understatement.

I'd set up the field for the team and then help pick up bats and direct players during practice and games. While it was fulfilling, it was also embarrassing. I was part of the team but not *on* the team and I struggled with what to do next. All my life, I'd dreamed of being a pro ball player. Now it seemed that I would never have that opportunity. That door was closing.

At the same time, my mother and I were working on passing legislation that would require insurance companies to cover medical formula for people who needed it and could not afford the high cost. We spent quite a bit of time at the legislative hall in Tallahassee working on this initiative which was later signed into law. It was fulfilling, but also exhausting, because I was trying to balance school and this important issue. We refused to give up and were proud to see that legislation passed into law in 2019.

Baseball, however, was my passion, and outlets just like it had been the way I dealt with my situation because I didn't cope with my diagnosis well, not until I got older and came to faith. Our family even sought out counseling after first finding out I had EoE, but I felt like it was a waste of time at that age because it seemed no one really understood what I was going through. I poured everything I had into baseball to feel more 'normal' and act like I had a normal life.

In the end, even after years of can-do perseverance to make it onto the team, baseball was gone, along with the identity and the future I had dreamed of.

I realized my mindset needed to change.

Dwelling on what wasn't going to be would only make it worse. I couldn't keep skipping classes and avoiding adulthood either, so I decided to get a job to help pay some of my college expenses, give me some spending cash, and to feed and care for my new dog, Bentley. Not to mention, as something to do in those long, empty hours baseball no longer filled.

It was easy to feel like I'd failed when I didn't make the team, but if there's one thing you learn in sports, it's that failure is all part of the game. Sometimes, the conditions are perfect and you win. Sometimes, despite those same conditions, you lose. Either way, you keep moving forward, and that was what I had to do.

Of course, I didn't love the retail job at first. I don't think anyone loves going to work in the beginning, but it certainly grew on me. As I made friends and found my place there, I began to enjoy it and see the value of helping customers and coworkers every day. These were people with joys and difficulties just like me, and they quickly became the people I could share a smile and a laugh with. It also got me out of that self-focus.

The whole time I was at VSU, beginning with the very first day in my dorm room and all the way up until I moved into my apartment as a junior, my mother had been mailing me books and messaging me video sermons from her studies. Many of them.

I often just tucked them into a dark corner on my bookshelf or my phone to the 'Never Read' pile, with no clue they would ever go to good use.

It wouldn't be until another situation arose with my mom that I felt the willingness to listen because, even though I always believed that everything would turn out fine for her after she received her own diagnosis, I didn't have any hope for a better future for myself.

Not yet.

Stephanie

As a mom of boys, I've had my fair share of scares. One time, when Dalton was just three, our family stopped at a builder's open house to look at a new build. We'd been engrossed in our conversation with the salesman for a few minutes when I looked around for my oldest son, and I realized Dalton wasn't there.

He had found the site's golf cart, gotten behind the wheel, and was driving it directly toward a very busy road.

My maternal instincts kicked in and I took off running, leaping over a hedge of bushes and jumping onto the cart to stop it, like some kind of scene out of a movie. I honestly don't know how I accomplished this because I was wearing a pencil dress that didn't allow a lot of room for feats of jumping. I firmly believe God's angels helped me over those bushes and into the cart in time to stop Dalton from getting hurt.

My love for my boys is unconditional and doesn't stop no matter what happens. It comes before everything in my life and fuels me to do things like leap onto a moving golf cart. God's love for all of us is like this—unconditional and more powerful than we realize.

Since the writing of *Home Plate*, our family has learned so much more about God and His Kingdom. We now know it wasn't God who gave our son a disease. God, in His infinite goodness, wouldn't do that.

God's ultimate desire is for us all to be well and, in His eyes, we are already healed—if only we begin to see His perspective.

Because I hadn't fully immersed myself in the Bible or dedicated time to study scripture, I wasn't fully aware of this and of God's message to us. I didn't know the truth about how Remington could be healed because I hadn't invested the time to learn it through the Word.

Like many people, I attended church every Sunday and I'd been a Christian since my teenage years, but I had never heard what living scripture meant for us and how it could transform our lives. I didn't learn these things for a long time in my faith journey, until I had that cancer scare.

When I had a breast biopsy in 2017 and was told that it was cancer, I was absolutely stunned. This was the "Big C" that ended many people's lives. I remember getting down on my knees and thanking God, promising I would be a light for Him throughout this struggle to show others His love. That, I later realized, was another prideful statement. Not meant in a prideful way at all, just focused on the wrong lesson. My wrong thinking!

Physically, I changed my diet to eliminate sugar, becoming more mindful of what I consumed. I increased my intake of vegetables and fruits to treat my body like a temple. I also started practicing yoga and prioritizing self-care. But as I began to be healthier inside, spiritually, I struggled with anger towards God. I also began to do a really good job of feeling self-pity.

I remember saying to Him, "Okay, God, I guess I haven't learned the lessons that you've been trying to teach me, and so you picked me? Out of all the people in this world, why me again?"

I yearned for guidance and solace from anywhere or anyone that knew anything. I started researching breast cancer and related treatments, reading into the various options available while I struggled with what to do.

Although doctors will advise against relying on the Internet, I couldn't resist the urge to educate myself about what I was up against. I wanted to know the impact of radiation on my quality of life and wondered what chemotherapy would entail. I made sure the sources I found were reputable, backed up by scientific studies and real-world examples. I didn't want to make a decision based on hearsay or "junk" science.

I confided my fears to Mike, uncertain about the path I should take. During my consultations with doctors, we discussed the available treatment options, including the possibility of a double mastectomy followed by reconstructive surgery.

How will my family be affected by all of this? What kind of stress will they endure? What would the treatment do to the rest of me? What will life be like without breasts? How will this change me? Change our lives? Will it even work?

Thoughts of my boys and their future wedding days flooded my mind, and I couldn't help but wonder if I would be there to witness those precious moments. I wanted to watch them grow into fine men, to see their joyful union with their life partners.

I longed to live a long, fulfilled life with Mike by my side. Together, we had always dreamed of sitting on our front porch, listening to laughter across the yard, and playing with our grandchildren. There was great joy and happiness that awaited us in that cherished vision.

I worried about who would take care of my mom, who was getting older. Not to mention Remington and his needs— getting the formula, taking him to appointments, making sure he was okay. Life felt very fragile, and I wasn't sure I could take any more difficulty and stay feeling sane for my family.

Those "what-ifs" kept fighting to dominate my thoughts, just as they had with Remington's diagnosis. The loved ones I knew who'd been through this before had some devastating side effects.

When I was young, my dad's radiation treatments took a huge toll on his health, yet he was always so determined to go to work, despite his illness. That was inspiring and heart-wrenching. There were days when he had to work from home because of his fatigue and I'm sure that frustrated him, but he was also lucky that my mom was always there to care for him. With time, my dad recovered and entered remission.

This period brought my parents closer to God, and I remember spending countless hours outside of school at church. Their unwavering faith in the Lord was the foundation of my own for many years; but now, faced with an uncertain future, I found myself worrying, rather than trusting in God.

That's when a long-time childhood friend (my best friend), Donna, reached out to me and invited me to visit with her dad and his wife. I hadn't seen her dad, Don, since I was thirteen and was excited when I accepted the invitation. Having lost my own father years earlier, I looked up to Don and was curious as to what he could tell me that I didn't already know.

There were plenty of people around me who'd said the usual platitudes: "We're praying for you," "God heals all wounds," "Believe and you shall receive." I was skeptical about whether they were actually praying for me or just *saying* they were.

However, it was different when Don and his new wife, Sandy, prayed over me that day. They assured me that this cancer did not come from God and that, with faith, healing was possible.

After that prayer session, I knew I would never feel alone again. It was, without a doubt, a message from above, urging me not to live in fear of the words of doctors, but in faith. Don and Sandy didn't realize it then, but they changed the course of my family's life forever!

It's like the contagion effect when one person shares the message with another. Like dominoes. We can all be dominoes for each other by holding tight to the promises of God and sharing it with people who need it most.

In that irony only God can bring about, I realized that, for a while, I had been coming across sermons and teachings that echoed the same words they spoke over me. These were the words I became hungry for, and they filled me with hope like nothing had before.

To anchor myself in God's promises, I started writing scriptures and carrying them in my pocket. Reciting them became a daily practice. At first, I'd read aloud from my writings but, gradually, I was able to recite them from memory.

My mindset started to change, and I chose to believe wholeheartedly in my healing and the eradication of that cancer. Gradually, those beliefs became rock-solid, and I was no longer just writing scripture. They were true statements to my heart.

I began feasting on what the Bible said and listening to sermons by people like John Osteen and his sermons on healing. I listened to Dodie Osteen's testimony about her healing from cancer. I listened to Andrew Wommack and Gary Kessee, and I wanted to absorb and know everything if it meant peace for me and my family.

I started to seek out the things God specifically said about healing. The more I read and the more I listened to, the more my eyes began to open. The "veil" began to lift. Almost as soon as I began tuning in to these teachings, I began sharing these messages with Remington so he could experience the same peace and faith that I'd found and continued to grow in.

From the outside, his faith was strong. He was actively engaged in his youth group, even participating in mission trips and attending summer camp. His senior year came like a whirlwind, and he was baptized when he became a camp counselor. It seemed like he was on fire for God.

But he wasn't, and I began to sense he was distancing himself from God and from what I said.

When it came to my treatment, I consulted with the doctor and concurred when she recommended that I undergo a lumpectomy to remove all the cancer cells. The surgery was a success, but the recovery process was challenging.

I experienced pain that would throb at times. Eventually, the surgical wounds healed but I remained tender. Moving my left arm was painful and from shoulder to hip on the left side felt delicate. There were moments when I simply wanted to leave my arm hanging there despite the prescribed physical therapy, fearing the pain that movement might bring. Thankfully, Mike, Remington, and Dalton were there and cheered me on during every session. I couldn't have done it without them.

After the lumpectomy, I was referred to a cancer center for further treatment, and they sent me in for a radiology consultation. I sat there wondering why they had scheduled this appointment if the doctor already confirmed that the lumpectomy removed all the cancer.

That moment was one of the biggest tests for my new understanding of God's promises. I'd grown this faith from the seeds of these scriptures and these circumstances were now testing everything in me to see if I was rooted firmly. Thankfully, this time, I was.

That following August, the time arrived to send Remington off to college. I continued to share sermons and scriptures, praying for his heart to be softened and for him to truly hear what I was saying. I was so excited about what I was learning and its capacity for real and lasting change in my life. All I wanted was the same for him, but he wasn't listening. Yet.

I began to pray as if his faith was already restored. That was the mindset that got me through this cancer diagnosis, and I had faith it would do the same for Rem. I put a sticky note on the fridge saying: *Thank you Jesus for Rem's softened heart.* Each time I passed it, I would touch the paper and say the declaration aloud. My hope was for him to grasp the knowledge that I had now and to realize God's love lifted our burdens when Jesus went to the cross.

Chapter 3

The Principle of Gratitude

Remington

When my mother was diagnosed with breast cancer, I wasn't really listening to her conversations about God. In fact, every time she mentioned church it made me remember attending services as a boy, and I immediately stopped listening.

I hated sitting in those long church services, hearing about people who went through so much tragedy and how God was the One behind it. What kind of God does that? I could see it happening in my own family (my diagnosis and my mother's) and it made me question a lot of what I had learned. To be honest, I was done with all the God talk. I was pretty focused on my own life.

Back in 2016, the doctor had prescribed an inhaler to me with the hope that this steroid would counteract the eosinophils, balancing them to a normal level and allowing me to successfully eat food; and it did help, a little. I'd have fleeting moments of what it was like to be an average kid and college student, but I still couldn't go and get a slice of pizza with the other guys or sit in the dining hall with classmates over an actual meal. I would bring my lunchbox packed with shakes, but I was a long way from normal.

I was pounding fifteen to twenty elemental juice boxes every day to get adequate calories and nutrition. The college provided me with special accommodations because of my medical 504 plan (allowing schools to support students with disabilities) so I could have a bigger room to house all the shakes.

The boxes don't need to be kept cold, but they taste so much better that way. When they're warm, it's like drinking thick, lukewarm milkshakes. It was always difficult to manage room for so many of them in the fridge each day as a child, let alone now as a fully grown adult with EoE.

After a new shipment arrived at my parents' house in Tampa, they would make the three-hour trip to Valdosta and, using a wagon, we transported the nearly twenty full cases of shakes (each case containing about thirty individual shake boxes) up to my dorm room.

When someone asked about the hefty wagon while taking the cases up, to avoid many questions or having to give long-winded answers, I politely told them they could find my story on Google. There were multiple news stories and articles about our family and EoE, and this was just the easiest if I was having a tough day or didn't want to give them the entire play-by-play.

Other times, I would share my story because I knew that people were struggling with their own diseases or situations, or they had loved ones who were struggling and could find some hope and solace in what our family had gone through. We wanted people to see that, no matter the struggle, we can all persevere.

That was a big reason why we wrote the first book, and I distinctly remember dozens of conversations with people who had read it and been moved by our journey.

I also kept trying different foods with the inhaler as I got older. Some would end the same way all the other food trials had—me in the hospital for another endoscopy, another test failure, another recovery period, and then another trial. If nothing though, I was determined to eat, so we kept trying. I always thought that maybe this next time would be the successful time, and I wasn't giving up until I'd seen success.

I felt like I'd exhausted most of the food-to-try list when I finally decided to try plain beef while I was still in high school. To my shock, I tried a bite and could keep it down with no symptoms. *Wow.* This beef served as a glimmer of hope but, at the end of the food trial, we still had to have an endoscopy to check the results under the surface.

After traveling to Ohio, we were elated when the endoscopy and biopsies were both clear and normal. Finally! I had something other than shakes I could add to my diet. I could go out with my parents and get a plain beef patty or a steak and do the same with my friends. It just had to be plain because I was also allergic to most seasonings, except salt. I lost some of that excitement after a while because, when I looked at the bigger picture, it felt like a small win.

Those bites didn't keep the void in myself, that need for something more, from growing bigger and wider as I got older. I felt like now there was nothing left to try and fill it. I had already been to the parties, been to the bars, but it wasn't quite what I was searching for. I had no idea what I was actually looking for, only that there was this indefinable hole in my life.

When it came to my mom, I noticed that our conversations had begun to take on a completely different tone as her faith shifted and grew. There was a sense of authority in my mother's words, and it was evident that she was no longer afraid of her own struggles.

It took time (years, actually) for all of that to sink in and for me to begin to make the connection between that feeling of emptiness and what my mother was saying. I was slow to see the correlation that any of this could even help me, but I was quick to act once I understood that she'd tapped into something I didn't have yet.

She was starting to experience life as God intended.

Maybe I just didn't understand what she was talking about because I hadn't yet aligned my thoughts with the truths in God's Word as she was doing. I was dwelling on the instances where my long-ago pleas weren't answered and focusing more on my problems than on the solutions.

I had to prepare to dig deep, just like I did the year I had surgery on a labrum tear in my shoulder. That was my freshman year of high school and my doctor warned me I might never throw a ball again. I refused to accept that as my fate and got up every day before the crack of dawn to do the prescribed (and painful) post-surgery physical therapy sessions.

I surrounded myself with positive words, people, and affirmations. I did whatever it took to have a full and successful recovery for my shoulder.

Maybe, just maybe, I could do the same with my faith.

I felt that opening my heart and mind offered the possibility of more, for myself and my life. To a way of reconnecting with God, but in a way that didn't make me angry or confused but joyful, like my mother.

Isaiah 53:4-5 (NIV) says, "Surely He took
up our pain and bore our suffering,
yet we consider Him punished by God,
stricken by Him, and afflicted. But He was
pierced for our transgressions, He was
crushed for our iniquities; the punishment
that brought us peace was on Him,
and by His wounds, we are healed."

That verse from Isaiah was one I wouldn't come across until long into my path back to God but, when I really, truly read it, it completely changed my life. It wasn't about denying the reality of my illness, but rather about affirming my faith in the healing process. Affirming that we are healed, according to that verse.

I thought of the small bites of beef I had been able to keep down. Maybe if I took that mustard seed of faith that began like the first bite of beef, God would grow that idea in my heart, and it could lead to something much bigger.

Stephanie

The healing process from my lumpectomy had been challenging, especially for someone like me who is always on the go. Go-go-go was just how it needed to be since the day I became a mother. Getting the kids to school, getting the household in shape, getting to work while also accommodating everyone's needs, all with gusto and happiness, and all within a 24-hour day. I loved it.

As difficult as it was, though, in the end I knew that bedrest was best for all our sakes. I needed to get better as quickly as possible and stay focused on making a healthy recovery for myself and my family.

I had watched Rem go through his own bout of physical therapy with his shoulder surgery a few years prior and I remembered how hard he'd worked to make a full recovery. It kept me motivated to do the same.

It wasn't long after the lumpectomy that it was suggested I be seen by a radiologist. The day of that consultation, I wrote several special Bible verses on sticky notes and tucked them in my pocket to comfort me and ease my nerves.

However, as soon as the radiologist started talking, it didn't take long for the initial confusion over my being there to turn into undeniable shock. His words seemed to stumble out in slow motion as he told me I should have twenty radiation treatments on my chest as a precaution, just in case, against the return of cancer.

Wait, twenty? That seemed excessive. I struggled with why they wanted me to follow the treatment protocol of a stage-four disease when I showed no signs of it. After all my months of research, I knew the potential side effects well. Radiation could do irreparable damage to my organs…was that worth doing "just in case?"

I simply didn't understand the need for what I saw as such aggressive treatment in lieu of a successful operation. Radiation could treat any lingering cancer cells, true, but it could also have a negative effect on my heart and lungs. Why take such a risk if I was cancer-free?

Nevertheless, I scheduled the weekly treatments, went home, and started doing even more research. What I learned shocked me.

A significant number of women undergoing this type of radiation eventually lose their lives; not to cancer, but to heart-related issues or some other form of heart disease.[1] These numbers weren't something I could brush aside or ignore, and I didn't want to become one of those statistics, not after everything else I'd been through.

I prayed to God for guidance, went to Mike for support, and, ultimately, decided against the risks of radiation. In the end, nothing they said could convince me to agree to that treatment.

I wanted to do whatever would provide me with the greatest chance of being there for my family the longest. I trusted in the oncologist's report that showed me I was cancer-free. For me, not taking the extra radiation step was the answer.

So, I called and canceled all twenty appointments the next day.

I wasn't surprised when the doctor called me that same evening, expressing major concern. He warned me about how serious this decision could be and that, to be safe, the best treatment method would be to take the radiation.

Politely declining, I explained my feelings on the facts I'd found, that radiation is not a one-size-fits-all. When letters came in the mail from the cancer center, encouraging me to reschedule the radiation appointments, I ended up tossing them in the trash. I stood firmly on my faith that this was the right path for me.

---

1 Cheng et al. "Long-Term Cardiovascular Risk After Radiotherapy in Women with Breast Cancer." National Library of Medicine, 21 May 2017, www.ncbi.nlm.nih.gov/pmc/articles/PMC5524103/.

———————————

Please understand that I am not advising against recommended medical treatment. Each person has the right to make their own decisions regarding their medical care, and I chose what I believed was best for me. Your treatment path is strictly for you to decide. You need to do your research and understand all the pros and cons of your options. Where you are in your medical journey may not be the same place I was, and your treatment options may be different. Whatever decision you make, be sure it is an empowered one that you can feel confident in making.

———————————

For anyone going through any kind of medical challenge, I would encourage you to be in the Word of God daily and to stand on His promises. This was what provided me with a way out of darkness and an anchor of hope when I was first diagnosed, and on those tough days during my recovery.

I was blessed to have an incredible surgeon and stayed in gratitude that the cancer was removed. Keeping my body free of cancer was always my goal, so I kept up the healthy eating and exercise and continued reciting scripture over myself. I became laser-focused on the promise that disease had no right to exist within me.

Sometimes, the hope of meeting that goal became undeniably shaky when I'd feel a sharp or minor pain in my chest. The bleak possibility of death would flash before my eyes and I'd worry about who'd take care of the household, whether I made the right choice in saying no to radiation, and what my family would do if I was gone.

When those thoughts crept in, I'd remind myself that those thoughts were not from God and recited scripture over my body to convince my heart of God's truth. I'd go back to the scriptures that had given me so much strength and lean on them until my worries went away. There were times when those emotions were a roller coaster but, overall, my faith remained steady.

My family was also understandably scared. My mom often said, "I'm just worried for you, Stephanie." Of course, she didn't want to see her daughter suffer, just like I never wanted to see my boys in pain. We're both mothers, and we spoke from the same deep emotion of love. I told her I appreciated her concern, but I couldn't afford to dwell in fear myself.

I had already done that and wasn't going to go there again.

When Remington was young and we had no idea what his future held, fear consumed me. There were many days I'd find myself paralyzed by the thought of losing my son. Sleepless nights were followed by low energy, running on less than empty, and dark depressions. Doing my best as a mom and wife often didn't feel like doing enough.

We all have moments when we trip and fall or lose hope, and sometimes it can be hard to remember that God is with us and is there to pick us up and deliver peace and strength.

On one trip to Cincinnati when Remington was little, I remember feeling so hopeful that he had passed his food trial, only to face another crushing disappointment when the test was a failure. When we got back home, we received a letter inviting him to participate in a drug trial for a medication not yet approved by the FDA.

For a second, I felt excited at a new possibility, but that feeling subsided when I thought about the prospect of my child being used as a guinea pig. My son, who had already suffered so much, didn't need to go through more suffering. What if the treatment didn't work? What if it made him worse? I couldn't say yes to it. This felt like a dangled carrot that we couldn't grab, right after another devastating blow.

I sought solace in alcohol that night, losing myself in wine instead of turning to faith or to Mike. It's not a memory I look back on fondly. The day-after hangover left me feeling awful and vowing to never let alcohol control me again. I had allowed my frustration that God wasn't hearing my pleas to consume my thoughts and control my choices.

Going from appointment to appointment with my young son back then, it was so difficult not to let worries sow seeds of doubt which then grew into giant, overwhelming fears. It was hard to always be confident I was making the best decisions when it came to his treatments, to know if I was making the right choices for him, and now, for myself.

I stood firm in my no-radiation treatment, but I would be lying if I said I never had doubts or fears. When I wavered, I came back to a conversation with my lumpectomy surgeon, who told me she believed my cancer diagnosis was not a test or ordeal from God, but rather, quite the opposite.

She said that God only gives good things to His children. This cancer was in no way a trial given to me by God, and that I wasn't to blame Him for it.

God only gives good things to His children.
(James 1:17)

I kept circling around the word "good" and thinking about what it meant to me, and to what we had all been going through.

In my search for assurance over the years through Rem's diagnosis and my own battle with cancer, the realization, and more importantly, the bone-deep acceptance that God is kind, merciful, and only gives good things to His children was an indicator that I'd been going about this all wrong.

God never gave us these struggles to begin with! In that moment, I realized that mistaken belief had been why I was so full of fear. Back then, my faith wasn't based on the promises of the Kingdom, but on my worldly wants, desires, and pleas.

I was determined to align my thoughts with God's truth, His Word, to keep myself out of that fear mindset that it was so easy to slip into. If my inner thoughts didn't align with His goodness—as in, *I'm terrified, this is bad, what-if*—then they do not belong to me and are not coming from a place God wants me to be. 2 Timothy 1:7 (NKJV) says, "For God has not given us a spirit of fear but of power, and of love and of a sound mind."

It's up to us to embrace this spirit and use it to replace fear with trust.

In other words: It's up to us to have faith.

We have a choice in what we believe. We have a choice in what we dwell on. We have a choice in what we fuel our minds with and how those things impact us. Hebrews 6:18 (NIV) also says, "… it is impossible for God to lie…"

The realization of that scripture is profound! If God's Word is true, we can follow in full faith that He has our back and will provide us with power through His Spirit.

After that conversation with my surgeon, I no longer saw my purpose as thriving under suffering or my prayers as pleas. Instead, I focused on embracing my faith and hope in the healing hand of God, here and now.

I knew I had to tell Remington and Dalton about this revelation. I told them that healing could happen for all of us, even for Rem and his disease. I just knew that I *knew* that we were meant to experience all the good God has laid out for us.

This desire for healing quickly grew into a sense of hunger for more when I shared the same message with my closest friend and confidante, Donna. She and her family had prayed with me at her home just a few days after I met with the lumpectomy surgeon and, after sharing this news with her, both faith and hope reignited in me yet again.

At the beginning of my diagnosis, Donna's family had also introduced me to Dodie Osteen's *Healed of Cancer* booklet, a testament to Osteen's triumph over liver cancer, despite being given only weeks to live.

It was a true testimony of how she spoke scripture aloud and wrote down hundreds of verses on paper, posting them all over her home, her car, and in every room so she would be thinking only the thoughts of God to keep the negative thoughts at bay.

I'd been doing the same and it had made a huge difference in grounding me in the moments when I needed more faith, but it took time to build that faith and study what the Word of God said about healing. I didn't absorb it all at once.

I started by reading verses and listening to sermons about healing. When I heard an important message, I jotted down the related verses and went back to the Bible to physically source the reference. Then I began speaking the scripture out loud and soon, scripture was all around me. It was just what I needed. I believe this series of small steps changed my life and that it can transform yours as well.

That's a big reason why I wanted to write this book. My hope is to give people a touchstone to return to when they want to tap into the knowledge God has laid out for us in the Bible, as a testimony of the power God can have in our lives.

Speaking scripture aloud, both to myself and other people who need encouragement, has become one of the spiritual building blocks I lean on. Doing that has built my faith in standing against those fears. 1 Peter 2:24 is also a key scripture I stand on because it shows us God's promise that we are *already* healed. I'm using the past tense because that miracle has already happened with God!

Understanding the truth that God provides us good things and then learning that He has already provided our healing was unequivocally transformative for me. This is God's inherent goodness because His unwavering intention is to bless us, not burden us.

The past tense usage in this promise also shows us that healing is the completed work of God. Before we even ask, He has provided.

For me, this shifted how I view every challenge, every mountain. Any obstacle that comes my way is now met with a fierce assurance in faith of what God's given to me.

This principle also assures us that His gifts, including healing, are not dependent on our present circumstances but are blessings from a loving Father that we should reach out to in faith. Now my daily prayers and declarations are guided by this, allowing me to profess not only what I have faith in, but what has been divinely established for me according to scripture.

In moments of fear here on this Earth, I refuse to speak negative thoughts and choose the truth of scripture instead. I *choose* to believe the healing has already happened because God said so in His Word. Accept it, trust it, and believe it before it's ever seen.

We believe with our heart that God's Word is true, and that comes before physical healing can even begin.

I kept sharing similar stories with Remington. I told him again and again that God wanted him well. I continued to declare the sticky note I'd put on the fridge that said, *Thank you Jesus for Rem's softened heart.*

I did this so my heart and mind would see that this change had already happened, even though he was still struggling at school, and those difficulties were affecting his ability to hear what I was saying.

By the time 2020 arrived, an appointment with the doctor after a routine mammogram tested all of my strength. Although the harshest evidence of the lumpectomy was gone—leaving me with only a healthy, healed incision—the pain of recovery still lingered.

As the doctor's face took on a worried gaze, I felt around for the little piece of paper in my pocket, breathing out a verse in my head. I refused to allow the "what-ifs," which I recognized as Satan trying to steal my healing, into my mind.

I chose to rebuke any thoughts that came against the promises of God. I stood on those scriptures that I was healed, and on Nahum 1:9 (NIV), which states: "Whatever they plot against the Lord he will bring to an end; trouble will not come a second time."

I stood on His promise that this cancer would not return. I believed this and kept reciting scripture aloud to continually build my faith so it would sink into my heart, totally and completely. No matter what the scan said, God only wanted good for me. I believed that deep in my soul. Then I heard the doctor speak.

"There is cause for concern," the doctor said, and scheduled me for another biopsy. In the days between the scan and the biopsy, I kept repeating those scriptures, holding firmly to my belief that I was already healed. The only question left was whether modern medicine would agree.

Chapter 4

The Principle of Faith

Remington

It took me a minute, but I began to love my job in retail and settle into this more adult phase of my career. I had given up my position as the team's manager and had accepted that not playing baseball on the collegiate or professional level was simply part of life. There was another path ahead of me now, although I had no idea what it was at the time.

Around the same time in 2020, my mom went in for her annual mammogram. When she called later that day, she told me the doctors had unfortunately found another suspicious shape on the screen in the same area she had the cancerous tumors removed from a few years before.

As she broke the news, I realized her voice was different this time. She had this tone of authority and was confident when she said she would refuse the diagnosis and choose to stand on the Word of God instead of giving in to panic or fear. She had a firm belief that she would be okay.

She was also positive that the doctors wouldn't find the lump at her biopsy appointment the next week. This kind of response—especially from a medical standpoint—was completely foreign to me at this point. I didn't know how to respond to her. *Here we go again with the God thing. Refuse the diagnosis? What does that even mean?*

I didn't say those things to her because I didn't want to be discouraging, especially in the face of her strong confidence. To me, she was simply handling some very bad news very well. I didn't realize the root of what she was saying came from a new understanding of God.

Our family has always been glass half-full kind of people. I was aware of the chance that cancer could come back, but we did as we always did and all focused on the best outcome while we stayed strong for each other. While I still wasn't entirely sure what to make of her words, I was impressed by her response and the confidence she showed.

A week later, she called me and said she'd had the follow-up appointment. At her appointment, the doctor pulled up the scan and looked for the lump they'd spotted earlier.

It was gone.

I was dumbfounded. *It just disappeared?*

Yes, she assured me. It had. There was no trace of anything anymore.

I thought about all of the words of praise she'd spoken around the house, the scriptures she had been speaking, writing down and carrying with her, and the verses she shared with me over the past months; and now, this incredible news coming after her firm belief that God only gives us good things. Could that be true?

Because if it was, it could give me something I hadn't had in a while.

Hope. Hope for a new future, a better one.

You see, I had become complacent. I had accepted that this was my life, and that it wouldn't and couldn't change. If what my mom was saying was true, what could that mean for me?

I wanted to know everything, so I asked her for the teachings she'd been studying. She was eager to share it all again because she'd been waiting so long for me to be open to learning these amazing things about God. Things like He really loves us and only gives us good things, and that His Word is alive.

I dove headfirst into those teachings and got honest with myself and with the Lord. My mindset was: either this is true and it's going to work, or it's not and it's all a lie. Either way, the only way to know for sure was to educate myself and learn all I could. What did I have to lose? It was, at the very least, worth a shot.

It's not always easy or pretty to take a hard look at yourself and really evaluate what's going on beneath the surface. I was so full of everything but feeling nothing at this point. I had reached a crossroads and decided that I was done playing games and making excuses for myself. I wanted to see, firsthand, that what my mom was telling me was true.

I began listening to a TV series my mom had shared with me, and I remember being outside in the backyard of my little apartment, listening to one of those teachings from Andrew Wommack. At the end of it, they shared a testimony.

It was the story of the healing of a young girl named Hannah Terradez. She had battled a condition nearly identical to the one I had faced. She'd had a feeding tube, was unable to digest food just like me, and had been on the brink of death. Her parents were desperate for answers and by tapping into the healing power of Jesus, she not only survived, but she fully recovered and is now completely healed.

That gave me enormous hope in the fact that I could see myself being healed. It wasn't just an inkling of maybe I can be healed. No, I knew then that it was possible. This was an unwavering certainty that I *would* be healed, and that moment served as a starting point to taking steps in my faith journey. I rededicated my life to Christ and made the choice to start anew, allowing Him to teach me His truth. Not religion, not experience, but—*truth*.

That certainty, coupled with the complete healing and miracle I'd witnessed for my mother, provided the push I needed to transform my passive longing into active pursuit for God's truth.

For years, I had been so hurt and confused by religion and all the religious doctrines that I hadn't realized the answer I'd been rejecting was right in front of me all along. I pulled the books from the dusty corners of the shelf and started reading. I bought a Bible and began to study it.

A few things became very clear as I started studying the Word:

First, I found that God is incapable of lying (Hebrews 6:18). On top of that, God does not show favoritism or partiality towards anyone (Romans 2:11). Additionally, Jesus remains constant throughout time, unwavering in His nature and character (Hebrews 13:8).

Last, that Jesus healed them all (Matthew 15:30).

These revelations that God is <u>true</u>, <u>impartial</u>, and <u>constant</u> served as a strong foundation for my understanding of His will for my life—all of which is to be actively living in faith here on Earth, not passively waiting to get to Heaven.

With those few things in mind, I want to look at a moment in the Bible that eventually became the groundwork for my new walk with the Lord. This is what furthered my understanding of His will for my health.

In Matthew 8:1-4 (NKJV), Jesus had just come down from a mountain with multitudes of people following Him. Verse 2 begins, "And behold, a leper came and worshipped Him, saying, 'Lord, if You are willing, You can make me clean.' Then Jesus reached out His hand and touched him, saying, 'I am willing; be cleansed.' Immediately his leprosy was cleansed."

This man's experience of the power of God, all while he was enduring severe hardship and isolation, caught my attention. In that culture, lepers were deemed unclean and unwanted, often left alone as outcasts. Even more, they were not to be touched because people believed contact would essentially designate that person unclean themselves.

The moment Jesus touched the man, He not only went against all the rules and societal norms of the time, but he also chose to become "unclean"—a foreshadowing of what Jesus would later do on the cross by becoming sin (unclean) for us (2 Corinthians 5:21).

What did that moment tell us about Jesus' love and character? He is not ashamed of us, no matter what anyone says about me or you. You are not unclean to Him. You are a child of His who is worthy of being healed.

The leper also knew that Jesus had the power to heal, but he questioned His willingness; and this is how the majority of Christians view God when it comes to healing. If you ask anyone, even an unbeliever, if God has the power to heal someone they'd say, "Of course. God can do anything."

However, what the majority of people doubt is His willingness to heal. Maybe He'll heal *that* person, but would He heal me? Is something bigger at work here in the Word?

Yes, there is! Jesus didn't even hesitate for the leper. He touched the man and put his worries to rest immediately by saying, "I am willing."

God is no respecter of persons (meaning He does not show favoritism one way or another), and Jesus is the same forever, so what is true for this leper is true for you. He isn't showing favoritism in choosing who He heals, He isn't there one day and gone the next, and He isn't lying to us about any outcomes. He is, however, willing to pull us from our lowest of lows. We just have to reach our hand back out to Him and be willing to receive His help.

It is Satan's oldest lie and trick of deception to get you to question this about the character and willingness of God. Satan did it in the garden with Eve, and he's still doing it today. Jesus, aware of this, shows God's true character while here on Earth, and this story is just one example.

We also don't need to feel unworthy or ashamed when we come to Him. Shame is a feeling of helplessness or hopelessness in the outcome, like what the leper felt. That shame was lifted and set free when Jesus died on the cross so that we no longer have to carry it ourselves. Just like Jesus healed the leper and cast out this man's shame and sickness, He has done the same for us.

This truth was one of the first things the Lord showed me, and it became a guidepost for me going forward. I realized that if the leper was as worthy as any of us to be healed, then I was also worthy of healing.

However, the more I leaned into the Word and drew closer to the Lord, the more distractions I noticed vying for my attention. Social media, college, and the stressors of life can make it challenging for anyone to stay focused and committed to spiritual growth.

One of the biggest temptations I faced, then and now, was allowing those other things to get in the way of my time of getting into the Word. I had to make God's Word a priority and remind myself of what was more important in my life and in my heart. Whether it be from being busy or lack of routine, whatever it is, the enemy just wants to get your mind off God and onto something else.

I took the discipline I had used for everything else and applied it to learning and absorbing as much as I could. I wanted Him to be the root of everything I did and the highest priority in my life. My hope for healing was so strong that it was all I could focus on.

The television was switched off and social media apps were deleted from my phone. To this day, I still find it important to silence the noise of the world.

Once I did that, I began to see that constantly renewing my mind to God's Word and speaking what God says (meaning, speaking His scriptures out loud) was a great way to replace all the negative thoughts of this world with positive thoughts, which are strengthened by hearing the Word.

Romans 10:17 (NKJV), "So then faith comes by hearing, and hearing by the Word of God."

These teachings were also showing me that Jesus healed not just some or a select group, *He healed them all.* I had learned the exact opposite of this in church growing up—that God chooses who He heals, and that message never sat right with me. This meant there was a disconnect somewhere, something that I even felt was a mistruth, and again, I already knew God didn't lie. I needed to dig deeper.

The next story I came across made the message I sought crystal clear. It revealed to me that healing is for us all, and that He never turns anyone away, which meant everyone—every single one of us—can be helped by Him. It showed me the truth about God "choosing" who He heals.

There is a story in Luke Chapter 8 about the woman with the issue of blood. I spent a lot of time reading it because I could relate to this woman's journey so much, just as I could the young girl's testimony from Andrew Wommack's teaching. This story, along with the one in Matthew 8, was the most instrumental for me in the beginning. They changed my attitude, outlook, and understanding of God.

I encourage all of you to read these passages for yourself, to spend some time in prayer and ask the Lord the tough questions on your heart. He's a big God, and He can handle our questions. In fact, He wants you to ask. Even more than you want to hear the message, He wants to share it.

In Luke 8:43, the Bible tells us about a desperately sick woman who had spent every dime on doctors but hadn't found a cure for her illness. She'd been suffering from continuous bleeding for twelve years and was desperate for answers. Just as with the leper, the people in the town deemed the Woman as unclean.

They deliberately avoided her and refused to have any contact with her. She didn't enjoy the exchange of friendly handshakes, hugs, or the touch of other people. She led a life of solitude. I knew and understood the pain of that isolation. I was reminded of it every time I had to grab a formula shake.

When Jesus came to her town, she was confident that this man the people had spoken of would bring her healing since it was reported He'd done so for many others. Word of His power had spread far and wide and she'd wanted to know if this was indeed the man who had been talked about for so long. In fact, Jesus was so sought after that the Bible says, "the multitudes thronged Him."

Verse 44 (NKJV) starts by telling us that the woman, "came from behind and touched the border of His garment. And immediately her flow of blood stopped." Jesus replied, "Who touched me?"

Everyone around Him denied being the one to do so and Peter and his disciples said, "Master, the multitudes throng and press You, and You say, 'Who touched me?'" But Jesus said, "Somebody touched me, for I perceived power going out from me."

The power Jesus spoke of was the power to heal, provided to Him by the Holy Spirit and now, to the Woman. Acts 10:38 (NKJV) says: "How God anointed Jesus of Nazareth with the Holy Spirit and with power, who went about doing good and healing all who were oppressed by the devil, for God was with Him."

After receiving this power, the story goes on to say that the woman saw she couldn't be hidden in the large crowd and came trembling, falling at Jesus' feet, when she told Him what had happened. Jesus looked at her, as Mark 5:34 (NKJV) states: "And He said to her, 'Daughter, your faith has made you well. Go in peace and be healed of your affliction.'"

In Mark's full account of the story, Mark 5:25-34, he says that when the woman heard of Jesus and came behind Him, she said, "If I just touch His clothes, I will be healed."

The woman was sick and tired of being sick and tired, and frankly, she was out of options. She risked everything going into that crowd to touch Jesus' clothes. For her, there was no doubt that touching His garment would heal her.

That passage in Acts is also key to understanding why Jesus was able to heal her. He was "doing good and healing all who were oppressed by the devil, for God was with Him."

In Mark 3:20-30, Jesus is accused of casting out demons by being a demon. Jesus refutes this claim and states, (I'm paraphrasing) a house divided against itself cannot stand. That "house" is His Kingdom. This means that Jesus could not have healed this woman if her illness *was* from God, because God was with Jesus, who is the Healer.

Let's take that a step further and put the pieces together, as I did when I read these passages. If this woman's illness was from God, Jesus would essentially have been divided against His Father. Instead, He was doing the good that God had given Him the power to do.

When I was growing up, I was taught that God controls everything. That meant God could choose to give you a sickness and then maybe He'd heal you later. If not, at least you'd be better when you get to Heaven.

I learned from Acts 10:38 that Satan is the author of sickness and disease, not God. God is not partnering with the devil to teach you a lesson. He is in Jesus, healing those who have been oppressed by the devil. The scriptures on this are very clear.

With that and the story of the Woman, I had to ask a hard question: *Whose choice was it to be healed? Did Jesus choose to heal her? Maybe God? Did Jesus' disciples pray for her?*

None of those.

The woman made the decision to be healed. Jesus didn't even know she was there, according to Luke 8:45. She decided to tap into the power that was already being provided through the anointing on His life; no one else could do this for her.

And then—and this is the part that was so key to me and made such a profound difference in my life—through her faith in that power, *BANG!* She was immediately healed.

What if I could experience the same thing?

We, as believers, already have access to His power through our faith, just as this woman did. Here's an analogy I heard from a pastor who explained this concept with such clarity.

When you walk into a room and flip a switch to turn on the light but nothing happens, what do you do? You might answer, "Check the lightbulb. Duh." But why would you start with the lightbulb?

Because you know the power has already been supplied by the power company and it's up to you to cooperate with the laws that govern electricity, whether that is by flipping the switch on or by changing the lightbulb, right?

Let's say you flip the switch and nothing happens, so you call the power company and say, "My light isn't working, please come and fix it!"

The power company isn't going to rush over in a truck. Instead, they will check the connection from the power grids to you, see that it is working, and then ask you to check that the lamp is plugged in, the breaker hasn't tripped, and that the lightbulb is intact.

Many believers do the same thing with God. They pray and beg God to heal them or to fix their situation when, all the while, the power has already been supplied.

1 Peter 2:24 (NKJV) says: "Who Himself bore our sins in His own body on the tree, that we, having died to sins, might live for righteousness–by whose stripes you <u>were</u> healed."

Notice how the scripture is written in the past tense, *you were healed.*

Jesus already supplied all the power for our healing on the cross when He died for us. We just have to decide whether we are going to believe it and receive it, (the connection) or not.

In the same way there are natural laws that govern electricity here on earth, there are laws in God's Kingdom. Faith is one of those laws. We activate the promise of healing by being fully persuaded (faith) that it is God's will that we be healed, and that Jesus purchased it for us on the cross.

Faith is the switch, but Jesus can't flip it for you. You have to have faith that the power is there and flip it on yourself.

After two decades of dealing with EoE, I was at a point of a deep, overwhelming desire for healing in my own life. I wanted to see the same miraculous change as the woman with the issue of blood. I realized the only way to get there was to continue to renew my mind to the Word of God to the point where I was fully persuaded and could flip the switch in my own life. I had nothing to lose, just like her; no reason not to believe in God's promises, and not to take this leap.

My mom had also been declaring her healing through scripture, confessions before her appointments and in her everyday life, and this had incredible consequences. I could see, literally with my own eyes, how her deep faith had changed her health. I wanted to do the same. I knew I needed to change the lightbulb, meaning my own thoughts, in order to do this.

I leaned on the scriptures that talked about healing. I recited them to myself out loud daily because I wanted to renew my mind to the truth in God's Word by *hearing* His words.

Not because this was a special, secret formula, but because it seemed practical to me based on what I read in Romans 10:17 (NKJV): "So then faith comes by hearing, and hearing by the Word of God."

I started listening to more podcasts and sermons about God while soaking up as much as I could. I was hungry for knowledge, connection, and a stronger faith. The scriptures started to come alive as I read them, and I got stronger in my belief of my authority in Christ and was baptized in the Holy Spirit.

Then, my faith wasn't just showing around me; it was *in* me and growing.

I also spoke as if I was already healed from the EoE...but was I? Would God really do the same miraculous thing for me as he had done for the woman, for the leper, for the young girl, and for my mother?

I studied more to understand these stories and to see myself the way God sees me.

After I rededicated my life to Christ, I immediately stopped swearing, which was a huge shift. It was as if the desire to swear was just wiped away. I used to be a frequent user of colorful language, but now I was able to maintain politeness, positivity, and carry on a conversation with others without feeling the need to curse every other word.

My mindset shifted, too. I started to think about baseball as something that had provided me with life lessons instead of something I couldn't have. I started thinking about the times I enjoyed birthdays and Christmas dinners with my family in gratitude instead of inner rage. I was able to think about a fridge of food in my apartment one day and finally believe I could have this for myself. Most of all, I chose to throw out all the old teachings and start believing God at His Word.

It was a dramatic shift and set me apart from the rest of my peers because I was no longer going out partying; I was driven to study the Word, doing whatever I could to strengthen my faith journey if it meant healing and happiness.

It felt a little isolating in the beginning because I wasn't scrolling for hours on a feed anymore, talking about the things I used to talk about, doing the things I used to do, or worrying about what others thought of me. Instead, I began sharing the material I was studying with my best friend, Chase. Our discussions became another way for me to receive that daily bread from the Lord and be encouraged.

I had met Chase years earlier at work. In the beginning of our friendship, we talked about sports, stats, and the job—nothing out of the ordinary for two guys. After sharing with him about what I was learning and how I believed in God for my healing, I could see that he was curious. I let him know about my newfound goal to learn everything I could about the Bible, and he shared with me that he was also on his own faith journey.

We began discussing our individual studies on God's Word and how He was at work in our lives. I don't know if there were any snickers or judgment from other people at work about us discussing the Bible, but I was thankful for this brotherhood and common ground. It was a connection I hadn't had with anyone else before.

After a while, I stopped caring about what others thought and focused instead on how I could help them throughout their day. I didn't really care that I was being vocal in my faith or spending so much time deepening my relationship with God. I had been transformed by reading about different stories, like the woman with the issue of blood, and it had ignited a want so deep in me, I could barely describe it.

Those stories had given me real *hope*. Reading about God's miraculous healing, and then seeing it in my own mother, had proven it was possible. Maybe my healing would be different; maybe it would be the same.

I didn't know and I didn't care. All I wanted was to have the same undeniable faith that the woman and my mother had. That alone could change me and my life.

I knew I was growing closer in my relationship with God because my prayers were different, too. I started to speak in gratitude and ask for guidance, even when long days were tough. It got easier to see God at work in my life and believe that He was really there for me.

One night, I had a moment that left me so shocked and amazed that I didn't fully realize its impact on my life until sometime later. It showed me that very truth I had been reading about for so long.

I had gone to bed before sunset because my shift started at 4:00 am. Daylight was still peeking through my curtains, so I covered my face with a blanket to block out the light.

Suddenly, I felt a change in the room's atmosphere—the air grew cooler, crisper, and cleaner. It was as if someone had just exhaled a minty breath in my direction. A little puzzled, I thought, had the A/C broken? Was the window open?

I didn't ponder over it a whole lot. I simply laid there and breathed in this clean, cool, refreshing air.

Then, I saw something out of the corner of my left eye. A blue swirl that widened and widened. I thought maybe with having the blanket over my eyes, that they were playing tricks on me, but as the swirl continued, it began to show the silhouette of a man.

The man's silhouette grew tall, rising from the bottom of the swirl. He said, in an audible voice, "You've always been healed."

Almost as quickly as it'd happened, the swirl and the man disappeared and the air went back to its original musty and humid state, usual for a summer in Georgia. I knew something, or someone, had come and gone because I could feel the change in the atmosphere.

The words kept echoing in my mind. *You've always been healed. You've always been healed. You've always been healed.*

They were almost the same words I'd been meditating on and declaring over myself for weeks. I knew that couldn't be a coincidence. However, I had never had any kind of vision or encounter with God before. I wasn't even sure if that was what had happened.

In the end, I sort of brushed it off, went back to sleep, and back to my life. It wasn't until about a year later that the true understanding of that moment hit me, and the Lord showed me He'd done that to encourage me.

When I think about that moment now, I have to chuckle. You'd think that I would have been so excited, I'd sprint out of the room to tell everyone who'd listen about what had happened. I didn't. But I did tuck it away and kept on studying the Word.

That gentle moment from the Lord ministered to me greatly. He was showing me the power and encouraging me to flip the final switch. He was telling me what I was beginning to believe in my soul.

My healing had already taken place.

Stephanie

When I went in for the biopsy after that routine mammogram, I was firm in my faith. By now, I had had years of building my trust in God and His promises and I could feel the Lord's strength empowering me as I waited for the results.

I felt some nerves, yes, but overall, I held firm in the words I had read in the Bible, the conviction that I had that I was already healed, and that the lumpectomy back in 2017 had removed all the cancer. I had come to the point where I refused to allow sickness the right to exist in my body and I was done agreeing with any fear. That confidence got me through the mammogram and would get me through this biopsy.

A few days before the biopsy appointment, a friend invited my husband and myself to a healing service in northern Georgia. Mike had also been grappling with health issues and we were both looking to understand the anointing of God that we'd heard of. I thought it was the perfect time to experience what this fiery revival of healing was about.

The sermons were amazing, but it was the rebirth moment we had in a healing pool that had the most profound effect on me. As we both entered the cool pool of water, I felt a deep, abiding peace wash over my body. Every step forward increased that peace, surrounding me as if it were the water itself. In that moment, I knew with absolute certainty that the scheduled biopsy the next week would reveal nothing. No cancer would be found.

The night before my appointment, I continued my go-to practice of reciting healing scriptures and singing praise songs to worship God. I felt confident the next morning when Mike drove me to the medical center and waited in the reception area while I was taken to another room.

Every time my thoughts tried to race away, I'd recall that sense of peace from the retreat and from the knowledge I now had about God. As I lay down on the table, I remained calm and steady.

My sticky note scripture for this appointment was a simple one, Nahum 1:9 (NIV). "Whatever they plot against the Lord He will bring to an end; trouble will not come a second time."

This was to reinforce my belief that cancer had no place in my body, not again.

I recited that verse aloud as the radiologist technician began the procedure. After a moment, it was clear she was struggling to locate the concerning spot seen on my mammogram.

A few minutes later, she left the room and returned with the head radiologist. They repositioned me and tried again but could still find nothing.

The doctor shook his head. "We can't seem to locate the area of concern. There is nothing there, Mrs. Walls. We could check again—"

I smiled. "I know there's nothing there. I have a deep faith that I am healed, and I just know I am."

When the doctor said,
"there is nothing there," I knew instantly
there was no cancer in my body.

The doctor suggested performing another procedure with 3D technology, but I declined. I knew the spot of concern was gone. I had felt it that day in the healing pool. I was at peace with my decision and firm in my belief.

I hurried out to the waiting room to Mike. He looked worried. "Is everything okay?"

"It's more than okay. The spot couldn't be found. Praise the Lord! Hallelujah!"

Throughout the day, I shared my testimony of God's promise wherever we went. The grocery store. The gas station. People would embrace me and then recount their own experiences and testimonies. It was an impactful day in my life, and I hope in the other peoples', as we all reinforced our belief in the power of God's healing hand.

I know that day could have unfolded very differently had I succumbed to fear. If I had let the stress and worries invade my body or take root in my heart, I firmly believe that voicing my "what if" scenarios or saying, "I hope they don't find anything," would have invited the spot of concern to grow into something more. The negativity would have been an open door to illness.

There was a day, years ago, when the overwhelming emotions of dealing with Rem's illness hit me like a wave while I waited at a red light. I erupted in pure anger and frustration, questioning God as to why these things were happening. I struggled to comprehend the suffering that seemed to follow my family, causing chaos and stress as we juggled the responsibilities of managing two households, a rare diagnosis, and cancer.

I remember breaking down in tears and shouting at God while I sat at that light. I had spent too many years with the what-ifs, caught in the fear of Rem's diagnosis.

What happened that day at the radiologist, however, was different. It was all different *now*. I could see that healing was already here for me and for Remington. More than see—I could believe it in my soul.

That's not to say there are never any hard days. We're human. We fall and pick ourselves up again. There have also been moments that tested our calm and resolve, and even if my faith falters for a second, I take a moment to recenter myself and remind myself of the amazing power God holds when we understand the promises of the Kingdom. Thankfully, red light moments are few and far between, if ever, these days.

After the scan, I called Remington and told him what happened. I assured him that God wants him to be well and that he can experience healing, too, if he chooses to believe.

He told me then that he was ready. He was ready to listen.

I almost burst into tears. Finally, the sticky note I had written so long ago manifested into reality: *Thank you Jesus for the softening of Rem's heart.* God had moved and changed Rem's heart, from the inside out.

As parents, we have the power of prayer to be able to ask God to transform our children's hearts and bring them closer to God. It's important to learn about this authority we have in Christ because it can change a hopeless situation into an incredible manifestation, even for our children.

Now, that desired outcome, spoken hundreds of times over the years, had finally manifested. This has drastically changed our relationship because now we can talk about what we are learning and share our faith journey with each other, building one another up in encouragement and truth! It changed things so profoundly that we wrote this book together because our journey has been nothing short of incredible.

When I began to understand using my authority as a believer, I told Remington (and anyone who wanted to know) about an episode I once had with hiccups that would not go away, no matter what I tried. While I was tinkering with the idea that Christ's authority could apply to something as small as this, I realized I needed to muster the faith and actually *believe* these annoying hiccups could be resolved. I didn't want to put up with these hiccups anymore and I didn't need to!

So, I said, "Hiccups, stop now in the name of Jesus."

Amazingly, those hiccups stopped. The annoying hiccups were gone. I was astonished. A small feat but a feat, nonetheless. That tiny moment of resolve flowered into a fire of faith in the authority I had in Christ. I was so excited that I often shared instances like this with Remington.

Commanding those hiccups might have seemed silly then, but moving forward, when Remington would reach out to me for prayer about something as simple as a migraine, I knew he was actively seeking help from me and a reinforcement of his belief in the power of God through prayer.

One afternoon he let me know that he'd listened to a healing segment on Andrew Wommack's Gospel Truth, which told the story of a girl named Hannah with an eosinophilic disorder like his.

For Hannah's parents had taken authority over her sickness when she was young—just as I had mentioned about the power of praying over young children, taking our authority in Christ for healing. Rem was now an adult and responsible for his own decisions, his own authority in healing. He absorbed that message like a sponge and kept marveling at how amazing this story was, especially since she had a similar disorder.

This planted a seed of hope in Remington that he could now do the same, which was exactly what God intended and I had prayed for. That seed of hope, even for something as small as hiccups, would grow into a powerful faith as he dove deep into God's promises for us as believers in Christ.

That evening was like a fork in the road, and he changed almost everything in his life to match his faith. He started reading the Bible, praying scriptures over himself, and singing praise and worship songs along with me. He chose to disconnect from worldly music and TV shows, and he frequently called me from his apartment. We would spend hours discussing scriptures and their true meanings. His eyes were now opened to the promises of healing in God's Word.

I think of our journey again, like a mountain. If you have read Mark 11:23 (NIV), Jesus says, "Truly I tell you, if anyone says to this mountain, 'Go, throw yourself into the sea,' and does not doubt in their heart but believes that what they say will happen, it will be done for them." Believe in your heart what you want the outcome to be, and it will be done.

"Ask and it will be given to you; seek, and you will find; knock, and it will be opened to you." Matthew 7:7 (NKJV)

Rem was on a mission to move the mountain of illness from his body. Every single day, his faith grew stronger, and his conviction grew more powerful. He not only had to believe God could fulfill His promise, he must be confident it had already happened. This was a new way of looking at God's Kingdom, and it filled us with an incredible amount of promise.

"Now faith is the substance of things hoped for, the evidence of things not seen."
Hebrews 11:1 (NKJV)

Chapter 5

The Principle of Authority

Remington

That spiritual moment in my bedroom with God's promise that I was already healed was entirely transformative. My faith began to grow stronger every day, sometimes every minute, and that made me far more open to what God had to teach me.

As I kept diving into the Word, I began to find my identity in Christ when I was finishing my senior year of college. I accepted in my heart that, just as my mom had told me over and over, God is constant and inherently good, which flipped the entire way I looked at God and my faith.

I started to think: *If God only gives us good things, then He never gave me a disease. He had given me the everlasting promises of His Kingdom, and it was up to me to study his Word so I could grow even closer to Him and His will for my life.* I learned quickly that I had only scratched the surface of what God wanted for me—which was, ultimately, to claim my healing.

I'm certainly not saying that I knew (or know) all the answers the second I heard the message, or the second my mom was healed, but I did have a newfound and growing hope that was at the root of every choice I made.

To me, hope is the picture of what faith will bring to fruition, as Hebrews 11:1 says.

Once the idea that God wanted me well transformed into a belief, from hope into faith, my entire world expanded.

Faith served as the proverbial mustard seed and, as it flourished, so did my spiritual strength and desire to study. I began to read and hear similar testimonies of healing from diseases like mine and many others. I listened to these stories and wanted this for my own life, too. I began to believe it was possible. God's power knows no bounds, as demonstrated in the recovery of those people's testimonies, and now I had to learn how to receive this myself.

Before this, I used to think that this illness would forever dominate my life, but when I recognized that those pessimistic thoughts (*I will never eat again / Why is this happening to me?*) contradicted God's plan for me, I sought tools to defend myself against them and stopped speaking them aloud, as it says in Matthew 6:31.

I had to immediately stop those thoughts and not give them any more room inside me.

You can't stop negative thoughts from ever coming into your mind, but you can stop them from ruling over your mind or giving them power over your life by not speaking them.

Your words hold tremendous power. God formed the world and creation by His Word (Genesis 1:1-31), and everything is upheld by His Word. (Hebrews 1:3) And we, mankind, are created in His image and likeness (Genesis 1:27), so thus, our words are also powerful.

When you *speak* a thought, you are giving it life and releasing it into the world. It also doesn't matter if that thought is good or bad.

No one wants to give life to negative events, so why do that with your negative thoughts? This is why renewing your mind on a regular basis is so important. It reminds you to replace those old, negative thoughts with God's Word, which is life. Remember the lightbulb analogy? It's much like changing that bulb before it goes bad.

Anytime I felt myself trotting down a discouraged path or thinking about all the time I'd wasted so aimlessly at things like college parties, I remembered what I studied and refocused my thoughts. There was no point in dwelling in negativity or in the past. I was focused on a positive, optimistic future.

When we are driven and speak in worry, fear, or anger, we risk promoting the very outcomes we're expecting, as in the case of Job, as my mom mentioned earlier. Studies even note that negative emotions can lead to weakened immunity in our bodies.[2] I was determined to respect my health and honor God by keeping a positive mindset.

Not to say this isn't difficult at times. All around me, in the news and the conversations I am a part of, I hear so much about suffering, illness, disease, ruin, poverty, anxiety,

---

2 "The Power of Positive Thinking." Johns Hopkins Medicine, 1 Nov. 2021, www.hopkinsmedicine.org/health/wellness-and-prevention/the-power-of-positive-thinking

depression, and calamity. It is tempting to not let the weight of the world affect me. When I feel that happening, I firmly refocus my thoughts back to scripture and, in some instances, separate myself from those conversations.

Those experiences are actually a result of humanity's decision (Adam's) in the garden to choose the devil over God. When Adam transgressed in the garden, as in, when he and Eve ate the fruit from the Tree of Knowledge of Good and Evil, he relinquished the authority and dominion given to him by God over to the devil, who subsequently became the ruler of this earthly world, ushering in a broken, fallen world and a state of sin and death. (Romans 5:12)

In other words, he took his focus off God and His promises and chose to believe Satan over the Lord. Doing that cost Adam, and future generations, everything.

This sinful nature has been transmitted to every existing lineage of humanity, including me and you. This is why when Christians accept Jesus as their Savior, it is referred to as being born again or reborn, into a new life with Christ. You are taken out of one family (the fallen world) and grafted into a new one, as a child of God. (Colossians 1:13)

There are many religious interpretations and ways of thinking when it comes to this rebirth as Christians, but most will commonly note that sin is everywhere. There is also a constant temptation to listen to the wrong voice.

No one is immune to this, but you can shake off those thoughts by taking a minute to ground yourself. All it takes is pausing and reorienting yourself in God's Word. I stood my ground in the Word I was reading and listening to.

This message was brought home for me when I read Mark 4:14-20. In that chapter, it tells us how Satan comes immediately for the Word that the people have heard and that has been sown into their hearts. There are many reasons for Satan to do this, but a prominent one would be to prevent you from hearing God's message.

The devil is very aware of the power of God's Word and would like nothing more than to keep you from understanding that power. I stood strong in the Word so, when he tempted me with doubt and distraction, I spoke the Word of God back and recited scripture (actively replacing those negative thoughts with God's Word). Jesus did the same in Luke 4:1-13, when the devil tempted Him.

I refused to be distracted by negative emotions, painful symptoms, or the way I felt. Instead, I stood resolute in God's Word and continued to renew my mind to the promise. That belief grew bigger and stronger within me, replacing more and more of the desires I used to have that weren't from God.

Leaving those behind provided the space in my heart to fill up with the Truth and with a stronger belief in His promises. I knew that, in order to move forward with what I was learning and with embracing God's power, I had to first envision myself healed, nourished, and liberated from disease. Proverbs 23:7 (NKJV) says, "For as he thinks in his heart, so *is* he." I knew that I could not think I was sick because I would stay sick.

While I certainly think it's important to listen to what your body is telling you, remember that God is also there, saying, "Look at me, instead."

I didn't ignore my symptoms, but I chose to focus on the One who is my answer. I kept turning to the Word, over and over again, and finding more answers every time I looked inside the pages of the Bible, just like 1 Peter 2:24.

These words from God helped me make the mindset shift from *maybe* this could happen for me to this *is* happening for me. At the same time, I began to grasp my authority as a believer.

I also began to focus on each individual word of that scripture from 1 Peter. It didn't say healing is coming, or that healing is possible.

The Bible says clearly, we "*were healed,*" past tense.
As in, it has already happened.

I realized I didn't need to continue to plead with God to heal me. Think about it: if it's already been given, we need not ask again.

The healing is there, waiting for us to see it and see the truth.

God has provided the power all along. We need to see it, just as the woman with the issue of blood and the leper did.

This new understanding unglued my feet from the train tracks and put me on a new, exciting path. I was already well—what could that mean for my future?

I began to see that this body (my body) was not made for sickness. That, just as God had only good in mind for me, He also only has good in mind for my health. That realization changed how I saw my mother's faith journey.

My mom had been seeing the promise in scripture for years. Her words were building her faith and her faith had turned into inspired action. That action allowed her to visualize herself as healthy and well.

I thought she'd been so off-track the whole time she was singing and reciting verses throughout the house. In reality, she had been reinforcing the power of God over her body. She had been reminding herself that what she prayed for was already done.

She was believing in the past tense, just like that verse in 1 Peter.

Exploring the teachings of my now favorite ministers, such as Andrew Wommack and Gary and Drenda Keesee, helped me understand this further. I am profoundly grateful for their ministries, which provided a definite light to my path to genuine freedom from disease. Words truly cannot fully convey the love, joy, and appreciation I feel towards them.

I leaned on Andrew Wommack's "God Wants You Well" series many, many times. I was even further inspired when my family and I had the opportunity to take a trip to Ohio in 2022 and were able to meet with Pastor Gary from Faith Life Church. His discussions on our authority in Christ resonated deeply with me.

Through their words and the words of others, I realized many of us turn to God in pleading, or even negotiating prayers, to seek the healing we're looking for when faced with adversity or illness. I wanted to enjoy eating without pain, and I constantly asked God to heal me, but I repeatedly asked for healing over my body, hoping it may happen at some vague time in the future.

In Mark 11:23 (NIV), Jesus declares, "Truly I tell you, if anyone says to this mountain, 'Go, throw yourself into the sea,' and does not doubt in their heart but believes that what they say will happen, it will be done for them."

Note that Jesus says *anyone*, not just pastors or disciples or a chosen few, but all of us, can say to the mountain, "Move! Get out of my way!" (I'm paraphrasing). Our words are what release the authority of God's Kingdom here on Earth.

Those words also enable us to claim healing from our sickness, and we can tell the sickness or symptoms to leave, but only if we believe what we're saying and in the One who enforces it.

Galatians 3:13-14 (NIV) says, "Christ redeemed us from the curse of the law by becoming a curse for us, for it is written: 'Cursed is everyone who is hung on a pole.' He redeemed us in order that the blessing given to Abraham might come to the Gentiles through Christ Jesus, so that by faith we might receive the promise of the Spirit."

This is a powerful scripture, and it helps paint the picture for what you, as a believer, have authority over.

In Deuteronomy 28:1-68, God gives a list of blessings for obedience and a list of curses that happen as a result of disobedience (or stepping away from God as Adam did). At the time, in the Old Covenant, they had no intercessor and no atonement of sin through Jesus as we do today, so God gave them a guideline to receive His promises before Jesus paid the price for their punishments. In essence, God was saying, this is what will happen if you walk with Me, and this is what will come upon you should you choose to walk apart from Me. The choice is yours.

I encourage you to read Chapter 28 in its entirety. As you read, you'll see that the length of curses outnumbers the blessings, and you may think to yourself, "Whoa! God, this is intense and cruel!"

It's actually a display of God's mercy towards us. Since there was no intercessor at that time and sin had not been fully dealt with yet, God could not stop these curses from coming upon people as a result of their actions (disobedience).

Thankfully, there's nearly too-good-to-be-true news! According to that scripture in Galatians, Jesus became every single curse listed when He was cast upon the cross for you and me. Now we, as believers, are guaranteed those promises of blessings and are freed from every curse through faith in Jesus Christ. God put an end to it through Jesus.

Deuteronomy 28:61 (NKJV) says, "Every sickness and every plague, which is not written in this Book of the Law..." I personally believe that, while Jesus was on that cross, every single sickness, disease, cancer, and infirmity that would ever exist came into His body and He bore it so we don't have to.

Part of my belief in that, accompanied by the verse in Galatians, comes from Isaiah 52:14 (NIV). It says, "...His appearance was so disfigured beyond that of any human being and His form marred beyond human likeness."

This is talking about Jesus, unrecognizable due to the beatings, whippings, and the stripes He was given by those crucifying Him. He took the full punishment of sin in His body, which includes every sickness and disease. He took on so much, you couldn't even recognize Him by the end. Being redeemed from the curse (sickness and disease) means that we don't have to put up with those things when they try and come against us.

Jesus says in John 14:12 (NKJV) that, "Most assuredly, I say to you, he who believes in Me, the works that I do he will do also; and greater works than these he will do, because I go to my Father." 1 John 4:17 (NKJV) also says that "...because as He is, so are we in this world."

This is talking about Jesus.

In Luke 10:19 (NIV), Jesus declares, "I have given you authority to trample on snakes and scorpions and to overcome all the power of the enemy; nothing will harm you." Through Jesus, we are directly empowered to move mountains, claim our healing, set other people free, and so much more.

Here's another example of authority that I understood more clearly: Most of us understand how government laws work in our daily life. Gary Keesee told a story about a police officer who stopped a semi-trailer to explain how that correlates to the understanding of authority in God's Kingdom.

A police officer alone doesn't have the physical power to stand in the street and stop an eighteen-wheeler for an expired tag. The truck is obviously stronger and bigger than the police officer and could just run right over anything in its path.

The truck driver complies when stopped by the officer because he recognizes the authority the officer has (which is backed by the government). It's the delegated authority (from the government to the officer), not the individual's strength, that commands respect and compliance. God's Kingdom is the same.

Our authority in Christ comes from the institutional, unending, delegated authority of the Lord (the King and Head of the Government). It doesn't come from us alone. He is the One who supplies the power and enforcement (through the power of Jesus, living in us as believers).

We are the conduits of His Kingdom, releasing Heaven and its jurisdiction into this world.

Just as the police officer does not have the power to stop that eighteen-wheeler on his own, we cannot fight the devil on our own. We can only do it through Christ because, in Him, the war is over. There's no "fighting," there's only claiming the victory that is already ours.

Once I understood how to operate in this authority, I began speaking to the sickness within me, commanding it to depart in the name of Jesus. I was, after all, already healed, as He declared in the Word. I needed my body to come into alignment with this fact, too. I had reached a point where I hated sickness and disease—and then *declared it gone.* I had to declare what God has provided.

We all face the same enemy, the same one who showed up in Mark Chapter 4 to keep God's Word from entering our hearts. When you begin to believe God at His Word and claim His promises for something like healing, Satan is going to try to do everything he can to make you think that what you're doing isn't working.

He will try to get you off track. He'll come at you with negative thoughts and doubts that will make you feel like you're not doing enough—all to get your eyes off of Jesus and back onto your problem.

When you stand firm and don't waver beneath the devil's schemes, he has no choice but to depart. James 4:7 (NKJV) reminds us of that, "Therefore submit to God. Resist the devil and he will flee from you."

We are redeemed from the curse of sickness, but not redeemed from resisting the devil. Warfare is deception, and Satan's *only* trick is deception.

In the garden, Satan could not make Adam and Eve eat the fruit; he had to trick them into doing it. This is what you see with temptation today, a feeling of being drawn into something, whether it be pornography or drugs. That feeling of enticement comes from Satan because he needs your compliance, and through that compliance, he can enter and begin to steal, kill, and destroy.

Romans 6:16 (NIV) says, "Don't you know that when you offer yourselves to someone as obedient slaves, you are slaves of the one you obey—whether you are slaves to sin, which leads to death, or to obedience, which leads to righteousness?"

Based on the scripture above, we are, in essence, becoming Satan's slaves and opening our lives to him when we choose to willingly submit to that temptation of sin.

Understanding that could put the fear of God in you and make you never want to leave the protection of God's wing; however, we are all human and we will all sin and fall short. The good news is that if/when we repent and confess our sins to the Lord, that sin is completely wiped away and never remembered by God. It's already covered by the blood of Jesus. (Hebrews 8:12) If we do not repent and choose to continue in sin, we are riding a slippery slope.

My faith in our authority as believers was further strengthened when I read the story of the fig tree in the Bible. It's one many of us are probably familiar with, but I was able to see it in a new light after all I had learned.

After leaving Bethany, a village near Jerusalem, Jesus was hungry and saw a fig tree in bloom from a distance. He thought it would have fruit because figs are usually quick to sprout after new growth. But when he reached the tree, he found only leaves. No fruit at all.

In response, Jesus said to the tree in Mark 11:14 (NIV), "May no one ever eat fruit from you again."

The next day, as Jesus and his disciples were passing by, they noticed that the fig tree had withered from the roots. Later, in Mark 11:21 (NIV), Peter, one of Jesus' disciples, remembered what had happened the previous day and said to Jesus, "Rabbi, look! The fig tree you cursed has withered!"

I imagine His reply to Peter was accompanied with a slight smile. He used this moment to teach his followers about authority, reiterating that those who do not doubt in their heart but believe what they say will happen, will see it come to pass.

The second Jesus spoke to the tree, what was under the surface (the tree's roots), immediately died. This is a significant display of the Kingdom principle: God's authority. Jesus grants us the same exact authority to speak to and put to death these mountains in our own lives as well. I have seen this happen both in small ways and in big ones.

Around the time I learned about the power of speaking over specific situations and circumstances, my girlfriend, Jessica, and I were dealing with an issue with her cat. He had kidney issues that formed large crystals in his bladder. If you know anything about cats with these issues, you know it's extremely stressful for all parties.

I realized that the principles I applied to myself also applied to the cat, as one of the creatures in God's Kingdom. According to the blessings I'd read in Deuteronomy 28, I decided I would exercise my authority over him with the belief that those crystals would disappear.

I demanded that the crystals dissolve in the name of Jesus and that his body work and function perfectly and properly, just as Jesus demanded the fig tree to be gone. I believed that the root of the cat's problems would respond to the words I spoke because I said them in faith and used the authority of the name of Jesus. The next day, the vet was absolutely stunned that the crystals were nearly gone, but I wasn't. I was starting to see more and more how His Kingdom operates.

Another learning experience for me, funny enough, was the hiccups. I'd eat or drink something and I'd swallow some air and, as a result, I'd have the hiccups. My mom had already shared her hiccup story with me, too, so I figured I'd give it a shot. I decided to use this as an "experiment," so I'd say, "Hiccups, stop in the name of Jesus!" and they'd stop. Instances like this served as an encouragement going forward.

Know that the second you speak and exercise your authority in faith toward an obstacle, i.e., the mountain in your life (whether metaphorical or real), it immediately obeys. It doesn't wait, it doesn't linger. It is immediate.

That said, it might take some time for what is on the inside of you to manifest on the outside of you, as it was in my case. I knew the minute I spoke of being healed, it was done, but I felt nothing and saw nothing with my physical eyes for some time. I firmly believed that my body was aligning itself with the words I spoke. Behind the scenes, however, that mountain was already moving for me.

This is why it's important to know God's Word (His will) for your life, so you can know how to operate effectively in your authority in Him, and so you are not trying to exercise authority over something you have no authority over. For example, if you are married, you cannot use the name of Jesus to bring you a new spouse because that goes against God's Word. If you did that, you would subsequently be using the name of Jesus in vain and opening yourself up to deception from the devil.

By the time 2021 arrived, I was on fire for more of God's teachings. I continued to nurture my faith, all while still relying on the formula up to twenty times a day because I was not quite ready to explore a life without those shakes. I was curious about whether I actually could, but I knew I needed to build my trust in God's words even more.

It took me time to do that and to provide myself with this knowledge in God's promises. In fact, I'm still learning how to dive deeper into the Word and learn more of the truth. I still discipline my mind daily to align my mind, body, and life with God's promises of goodness, abundance, and wisdom.

I studied and studied, and a year or so after that encounter in my bedroom, I was on my way to work and listening to a teaching on healing when I was struck with the clear realization that I was already healed. Boom. Just like that. The seed planted the night I saw the silhouette of the man, who I believed to be Jesus, sprouted into active faith.

Acting on that faith when I got home from work that day, I threw the steroid inhalers into the trash and stopped relying solely on the formula. I saw myself as fully healed and eating food, and I decided to completely trust God and His Word.

I am not suggesting you disregard medical advice or ignore a diagnosis; rather, refuse to let it control your life. Turning a blind eye due to ignorance, not faith, will not yield any desired outcome.

When I decided this diagnosis wouldn't rule over me any longer, I chose to believe in my healing instead. I had gone deep enough into His Word to know that I have authority over illness, just as it says in Luke 10:19.

While my path may not be the same as yours, I encourage you to build your faith before making any decisions regarding your health. Don't skip necessary medical treatments or ignore doctors entirely. Let the Word and the Holy Spirit guide you in your choices and continue studying and learning on your journey.

For months, I had consistently affirmed, "Thank you, Father, for my perfect health. Thank you, Father, for my perfect cells, perfect esophagus, perfect digestive track."

I spent enough years in hospitals and on medication and knew just about everything there was to know about my disease, which had been predicted to be a lifelong ailment. I had also heard God's promise that night in my room and had read it in the Word. I trusted God entirely.

I went shopping for groceries, started praying over my meals, and thanked the Lord that I was healed according to His Word. I reinforced my faith by studying the Word and showing gratitude to God.

John 10:10 (NIV) says, "The thief comes only to steal and kill and destroy; I have come that they may have life, and have it to the full."

I knew that sickness steals, kills, and destroys, and thus, it cannot be from God. God, unchanging, gives us only good, and Jesus came to give us abundant life, not bondage. Before all of this, I had attributed my sickness to Him, thinking that it was some kind of lesson or message from God. In fact, that contradicted His nature, so every time I sought healing as a kid, I was doing so almost in defiance. I was ready to do things differently going forward. Doing it God's way.

God desires you walk in health,
even more than you want it.

I have emphasized on multiple occasions, and will continue to do so, my eternal gratitude for the medical care I received and the elemental formula that sustained me throughout the years. I genuinely thank the Lord for bestowing wisdom upon humanity to discover such life-saving innovations. Physicians are partners in God's healing ministry.

And yes, God has already healed us, but as I said earlier, our body, mind, and heart can take time to catch up with and strengthen the faith in this promise. I needed to build a fortitude of faith and strengthen the muscles of my spirit to see the change in my body.

While I do not advocate for discontinuing medications or treatments without guidance, recognize that ultimate authority lies with God and His Word. There is nothing too difficult for the Lord to manage.

In 2 Peter 1:3, it is mentioned that God's divine power has granted us all we need for life and godliness. Through God's promises we can partake in this power. The responsibility lies with *us* to actively engage in these promises.

Just like the woman in Luke 8, and her grabbing of Jesus' cloak to heal her from pain and desperation, I chose to actively participate in the promise of receiving healing. I reached out and grabbed it with all I had left.

God's Word is infallible, and His promises stand true. Once I believed this in my heart and soul, I was ready to live a life with Him.

And with food.

Stephanie

I remember the day that I picked up the phone to tell Remington that the suspicious spots previously detected on my scan were gone. They had vanished! I'm sure if I'd been with him, I would have been able to see the light of understanding flicker in his eyes. I was strong in my belief that God did this for me, and now Remington wanted to know even more about everything I'd gathered over the past few years.

He possesses a keen eye for detail and a contemplative nature, preferring to take in information before acting. I watched him connect the dots between his own journey with mine, and this sparked hope in him. A hope which would later blossom into an understanding of God's nature and love.

When it comes to watching my sons grow, I still cheer them on so they know I'm available for them. I've always told them both, "You can do it!" whenever they attempted anything that was difficult, including Rem getting back onto a clear path with his faith. I tried to never hold them back and to let them come to their own conclusions about whether something was right for them or not.

Young minds are impressionable, and the words they hear from parents and other adults in their lives have a lasting impact. What I didn't know back then was that, as believers, Mike and I had the authority to rebuke Remington's diagnosis of EoE. I had no clue we could combat his illness with scripture and, instead, stand in faith. Had we known then what we know now, we would have rebuked his illness and declared our son's healing based on God's promises and the authority granted to us.

It dawned on me after some time in my own faith-building that I needed to release any guilt associated with the nineteen years Rem endured. I needed to let go of the burden I carried for our son surviving on formula. Romans 8:1 (NIV) tells us, "Therefore there is now no condemnation for those who are in Christ Jesus."

God only wants good for us, and as parents, we wanted the same for our son. That wasn't something to feel guilty about. Guilt is also not from God. Letting go of any of those negative feelings, I focused even more on scripture.

In addition to encouraging our children with positive words, it's important for us as parents to also lead by example. Our actions and behaviors have a powerful impact on our children, especially when it comes to matters of faith.

As my spiritual journey deepened with God, I realized the importance of this and wanted to be a positive influence, especially as I watched Rem embark on his own path. It was an exciting time as he discovered much of what I had just a few years earlier.

I dove into the realm of faith-based healing even more and started attending a church with my absolute best friend Donna, who shares my beliefs. For me, faith-based healing is turning to what the Word of God has to say. The more I focused on God and what the Bible said, the more understanding and clarity I had in the deepening of my faith. I was so excited to walk this path with Donna by my side.

She and I were born just two days apart, grew up in the same church, and attended school together, which caused us to face several of life's challenges as a united front. Our bond deepened as we discovered the divine promises of the Kingdom, but we faced another challenge when she went through the same thing I had just endured.

We hadn't been attending this new church for very long when Donna happened to be diagnosed with breast cancer. She told me that her disease was at Stage 2 and my concern skyrocketed.

Fear began to creep in over my concerns for her, her family, and the decisions she now had to make regarding her health. I felt quick flashes of worry about what her outcome would be and what her treatments would entail, and I was angry at this disease for robbing her of time.

I knew, all too well, the energy required to make the appointments and the hours spent between doctor's offices, so I worked hard to become like a horse with blinders (to block out any negative thoughts) so I could support her and only speak with faith. I wanted her to know what I knew!

When Donna and I had conversations regarding her treatment plans, I would sometimes lovingly fuss at her to hold onto faith in the outcome of healing. I wanted her to have a faith just like mine, but I know it was a scary time. Anyone dealing with such a diagnosis would understand those moments of fear.

While I was on a mission, fully expecting a positive outcome for her by way of faith, I realized after some time that Donna's healing journey was her own. Tapping into this authority required *her* faith to heal *her* body, not my belief! I had to respect the way that Donna wanted to do this.

See, God was meeting Donna right where she was, healing her in the way she needed. As soon as I understood this, I toned my excitement and must-do attitude down, realizing that she was already healed, as the scripture is written. It just had to be her that dug into the Word to receive healing—and she did!

Ultimately, coupled with her prayers and declarations of healing, she decided to go through chemotherapy, a double mastectomy, radiation, and then reconstructive surgery. And praise the Lord, today she is cancer-free! It was a glorious day indeed when Donna announced she had entered remission! His presence was surely around us that day.

God will work in many ways if it means His child being made healthy. Whether it's through our doctors, our diet, or our discipline, there are so many ways in which God meets us where we are in healing. This was another major moment in my life and in my walk with God as I saw His promises of healing manifest for my friend.

Prior to stepping into the Pentecostal church I attended at the time, I had heard many sermons with my family and done several daily devotionals, but I always had difficulty grasping the truth of God's messages when I read the Bible or heard the message.

My scripture readings left me feeling puzzled or requiring multiple scans of the text, and I still didn't have a true understanding of His words. I went through the motions of prayer without truly connecting with its purpose, and those were prayers that sounded much more like complaints and pleas for help, lacking true faith.

Now, here, my ears were opened. Now, the words rang true, and I understood them in my heart! Now, everything about my prayers had changed.

While this church was a sanctuary for me, a prominent support in my new foundation of faith, God had changed me, and I could now see. I could hear Him.

My fervent desire was to cleanse myself of sin and doubt, embracing all that the Lord had to offer. Engulfed by a passion for the Holy Spirit, I eagerly welcomed every divine revelation that came my way and found myself more captivated by the day, growing even hungrier to absorb every word. I spent hours listening to sermons on healing, replaying them while taking notes and revisiting key points from the sermon each Sunday. This was my personal study of the Word of God.

In reality, the more I focused on God, reading His word and listening to messages, the more I saw through His eyes to know what the words in the Bible actually meant.

It tells us this in Matthew 6:22 (NIV), "The eye is the lamp of the body. If your eyes are healthy, your whole body will be full of light."

What we focus on with our eyes, what we look at, we become. I had to make an active choice to spend more time in God's Word so I could renew my mind to the way He thinks of me: Healthy!

These days, I feel a deep connection to God, engage in heartfelt conversations with Him, and constantly want to know more about how to help others receive God's blessings for themselves. It's incredibly exciting to see how the Lord operates in my life and the many blessings He pours onto me and my family. I want others to experience His goodness because it's truly transformative!

A few weeks after I started attending the new church, I was sitting in the pews when I heard the pastor say, "If God is speaking to you right here and now, come seek Him."

People were invited to come forward if they felt led to receive the Baptism of the Holy Spirit, and suddenly, I felt God's hand guiding me to stand up and go to the baptismal pool. I stepped into the water and the immediate sensation of immersion was like a protective shield, suddenly covering me and giving me divine protection. It can be difficult to put into words the exhilaration, sense of peace, and the overwhelming love that embraced me.

This baptism marked not only a cleansing, but an empowerment for me through the Holy Spirit. I'd accepted Jesus Christ into my heart as a young girl, but this was a different type of baptism—one in which we come to Jesus to be anointed with God's power and have the Holy Spirit (source of power) move into us. I knew it was the next step and I was ready to receive those promises!

As soon as I stepped out of the water, I felt rejuvenated and renewed, ready to face any challenge with the firm belief that God was by my side even more! I knew that the Holy Spirit was living through me.

In tandem with the baptism, television sermons, and consulting my Bible to verify the scriptures I quoted, I fed my soul with what it so desperately needed. Witnessing the Word come alive and understanding it with this clarity was a new experience for me that I loved.

I have since started hosting a weekly women's Bible study where we support each other and focus on aligning our minds with Christ's teachings. We emphasize the power of our words and take authority over anything contrary to God's truth.

Each woman in the group is balancing family and life while also passing on God's teachings and nurturing the faith of their households. They come to Bible study with stories of the positive impact this has had, and I am thrilled my testimony of Jesus has inspired them. Without Him, there'd be no healing. No Bible studies. These were the fruits of firm faith. In return, they inspire me to be even stronger in my own.

It is possible to prepare ourselves and our children for a life rooted in faith and victory over the enemy.

In Luke 10:19 Jesus declares, "I have given you authority to trample on snakes and scorpions and to overcome all the power of the enemy; nothing will harm you." (NIV)

This same authority has been given to us as believers, after Jesus triumphed over Satan on the cross. We have been gifted the power to overcome any obstacle or sickness in Jesus' name, if only we exercise it with faith. (Matt 28:18-20)

Near Thanksgiving in 2021, my mother was diagnosed with lung cancer. Mike and I were in the middle of building a cottage for her and my sister to live in on our property when we received the news. It was difficult for all of us, but we continued with pure love and strength.

I offered my mom words of support, encouraging her to remain steadfast in God's teachings, believing that He would bring her healing and a long life. I had to concentrate on renewing my thoughts and staying in line with God's assurances, fighting against thoughts that tried to bombard me with fear. I continued to seek guidance from the teachings of Andrew Wommack or Gary Keesee on television when I needed a bit of a reminder or a boost of comfort.

Like the Bible says in Ephesians 6:11, I had to put on the whole armor of God to fight against the wiles of the devil. The devil will bombard us with thoughts of defeat or fear, but I couldn't allow those thoughts to take root.

I gently reminded my mom to align her words with the Lord's promises, encouraging her to speak about life instead of fear. She bravely chose to undergo radiation and chemotherapy, and I stood by her side in full support. I also provided her with healing scriptures to declare aloud, witnessing the miraculous disappearance of a tumor after these treatments, which filled us all with gratitude and praise.

Despite that initial remission, my mom's fear resurfaced, and she expressed her readiness to join Jesus in Heaven. I knew then that her heart longed for rest. Her body was tired.

Before she passed, she left me with a poignant moment, giving me a glimpse of the divine. In our tranquil mornings together, I would snuggle next to her, singing hymns and "Give Me Jesus." Every time she smiled; I saw the Lord's beauty through her eyes.

Occasionally, she would laugh and talk about seeing angels around us. She vividly described their joyful presence, frolicking and soaring in the heavens. Her words painted pictures of a magnificent, ornate table in gold and silver waiting for her, along with beautifully golden streets and angelic trumpets announcing her arrival in a place more magnificent than any on Earth.

Her desire for healing went beyond earthly limits and she craved a free existence in Heaven. Some may find it perplexing, questioning the value of my prayers in times of loss. In truth, it was not my prayers that held weight but the sincere prayers of my mother. She spoke her desires for rest with Jesus and He honored her request. Her spoken words guided her to her Heavenly home.

I was thankful for that time with her and the glimpse of God that she gave me. That glimpse was another seed that grew my faith in what I already knew to be true, and I began to search for more answers about the fruits of God's Kingdom.

There were several moments after my own healing that reminded me of God's power. One moment was with the hiccups and the second was with our dog, Hank Aaron, who had become extremely sick around the same time my mother died. We took him to the vet because he wasn't eating and had lost fifteen pounds. We were a little concerned because that was a lot of weight for a healthy dog to lose.

When we took him in for an appointment, the vet informed us there was a problem with his digestive tract and that there wasn't much that could be done for him. The thought came to me later that day to pray over him, just like it did with that bout of hiccups. I remembered how Rem had done something similar with the cat and knew our dog was also one of God's creatures. I wanted to command healing into his body.

I searched for a scripture to speak over him, and I found Deuteronomy 28:4 (NIV), which tells us, "The fruit of your womb will be blessed, and the crops of your land and the young of your livestock—the calves of your herds and the lambs of your flocks."

I laid my hands on Hank Aaron's belly after I'd recited the scripture, and I commanded his body to come into agreement with God's Word. I commanded the ailment to leave his body and praised the Lord for Hank's healing while I declared that scripture aloud for the blessing.

That was it!

After my prayer, I kept thanking Jesus that Hank Aaron was healed. It took several days for Hank Aaron's body to show signs of healing, but he was soon back to himself again. I share these instances because I was still learning how to use my authority in Christ at this point in my spiritual walk, but I had to take baby steps and that all started with, surprisingly, hiccups!

I had to believe that Jesus would do what He says He will do. If I couldn't believe that about something small (like hiccups), and I had prayed for something much bigger and it didn't work (like healing Hank Aaron), I may have questioned my faith in being able to stand in authority.

With my faith journey about the power of healing, every moment was like a little nudge from God. The hiccups, Hank Aaron, my own health scare, and now others'. It's quite amazing how those little steps of faith transformed my life and theirs. It's that mustard seed of faith that begins to blossom and build your confidence only in the glorious power of Jesus.

While Remington was diving in to learn more and I was getting more involved in the church and the community, I wanted to know more about the power of prayer. Many of us want to shout out a quick need and have it answered right away. Or we want God to give us a sign, especially when we are in distress.

We want to randomly open the Bible and have our finger land magically on the scripture that God needs us to see. Sometimes this might work, but often it's after a prayer of plea or desperation. What if we didn't have to wait until the point of breaking to reach out for hope?

I found that the more time I spent talking with God and reading the Bible, the closer I got to Him. The closer I got, the more the signs became clear and frequent, and the more evidence of healing happened in my life, just like it did with our dog. I knew that these moments were not just coincidental or a stroke of luck.

Following that clarity, I felt the same overwhelming peace I'd received when I walked into the water at that retreat in Georgia and the baptismal pool at this new church. It only became more constant within me, as God is true and constant! As the Holy Spirit flooded me with love and clarity, my reassurance in God's divine operation only grew.

While I was aware that difficulties like cancer and financial hardship, or even worries as a mother, would remain for many people, this peace gave me the ability to see there is a reason to celebrate in every moment! Jesus is the reason, and He calls us to celebrate the blessings He provides through gratitude and prayer as we aim to grow with Him.

I believe that there is always room to grow with Jesus, and prayer is the only two-way communication channel to do so. It's also how we receive healing, prosperity, wisdom, and direction from the Lord. Prayer is so powerful!

That's why it was certainly a sheer joy when Remington called to tell me he was choosing his faith and that he knew that God wanted him healthy. He'd prayed over his body to receive healing and commanded his body to align with the Word of God. He used his authority in Jesus! He told me that he'd thrown away his inhalers and was going to do the same with the formula because he knew that his body was made to eat food.

What a celebration! This was the power of prayer!

Chapter 6

The Principle of Power

Remington

The incredible realization I had before throwing away my inhalers was one of many lightbulb moments that flickered throughout my faith journey, as God revealed more to me each day. Those moments were always powerful and came when I least expected them.

Part of the mindset renewal I'd experienced was working on my ability to stop focusing on myself and my own issues and think more about my impact on others wherever I went, whether that was to the grocery store, or work, or simply crossing the street. This was especially important to me because I know some people may never step foot in a church, so this encounter with me may be the only meeting they have with someone who knows Jesus.

As one of my favorite ministers said, "The only Jesus some people may see is the Jesus in you and the Jesus in me."

Most days on my way to work, I listen to a book or podcast that delves deeper into what I'm learning about God. In one particular episode on healing, I heard something that struck me:

"As long as you put up with being sick and tired, you'll stay that way."

I rewound and replayed that sentence. The second time I heard it, everything seemed to stand still for a split second. I realized that person was so right. I repeated the line in my head a few times and realized that there was a small piece of me that still believed the EoE existed within me, even though I'd been speaking to the illness in my body and building my faith.

It was right then and there that I was done with it. It was time to let go of the last of *anything* in my body other than God. I knew if I continued to tolerate the illness any longer, it would continue and persist, and I didn't want to depend on shakes and steroids for the rest of my life. I was done putting up with EoE.

I had had so many instances where I could see God's power over my life, dealing with my symptoms, even over Jess's cat, that I knew I had to make one more declaration to God to cement that trust in His goodness and my full belief in His Word.

"God, I know you've aligned my cells to function perfectly," I said out loud, "Just as You say in Your Word, I know that I am healed. I know that your promise is true and constant and that the EoE is gone."

The minute I finished those sentences, nothing instantaneously happened. There was no tangible feeling, no miraculous presence, but my mind had finally come into alignment with what was already in my spirit, and I released those words in full assurance.

I screamed as loud as I could, "I'M HEALED!"

It wasn't a scream as in an *aha!* moment; it was more of a declaration, said with authority. I was convinced I was healed. My purpose, path, and identity in Christ became clearer day by day as the things I'd been learning were right in front of me to see. These miracles were no longer just stories I read about other people. They were happening to me.

The level of clarity I gained made me feel brand new, and if I could have bottled it up to share with others, I would have. By writing this book, I'm doing the next best thing. I'm becoming a witness for the power of faith and trust in God's goodness. However, it's up to you to fill your own cup with Jesus.

When Jesus died on that cross, he died for our total freedom of spirit, soul, and body.

The proof of these promises is right there in the Word; just take a look at Isaiah 53:4-5. The punishment endured on the cross is what provides us peace. Jesus already paid the price for the hurts, the burdens, and the sorrows (in my case, the EoE), and He calls us to give those over to Him as soon as they affect us.

I started eating simple foods at first, easing my way back into the world of eating three meals a day. Instead of drinking the formula twenty times a day, I'd drink twelve and have one meal, then the next day, I'd drink eight and have two meals. After a couple days of doing formula and food, I transitioned to solely food with no formula. The more I ate, the more it confirmed what I had already known. I had no symptoms, no pain, and could eat anything I wanted.

Prior to this, I already had my yearly checkup scheduled at Cincinnati Children's Hospital for the summer of 2022. This was the same Ohio hospital I had visited countless times since my initial diagnosis. I needed someone to go with me as I needed to go under anesthesia for an endoscopy. My mom and I flew up together, as we had so many previous times. My support on every one of those trips had always been my mom and dad, and it was exciting to be there together since we were also walking our faith journeys together.

When we were in the examination room, the doctor asked me how I'd been doing. I told him that I was great. "In fact, I've been eating solid food for two months and I haven't had any pain or symptoms."

He was stunned. "You have? How? What are you doing differently?"

I spoke the truth that my heart had then known for months. "I'm choosing to believe what God says, and He says I'm healed."

I told him I'd stopped drinking the shakes entirely and I saw an expression of shock on his face that I'd never seen before. He wasn't as convinced of my healing and recited a long list of the negative side effects that could happen should I choose to continue eating food without the help of steroids. He encouraged me to confirm my full recovery with medical tests, even as he doubted it. It didn't matter. I knew my body, and I knew the power of the Lord.

"With all due respect," I said, "I respect your opinion and where you are coming from, and I'm thankful for your guidance. I know you're required as my doctor to give me these warnings, but I am choosing to stand on God's Word and His promises, and He says I'm healed. He has the final say in this matter and you're going to see the results of that today."

He didn't disagree. Instead, he just said, "Okay, well, let's take a look."

My mom came into the recovery room later just as I was starting to come out of the anesthesia. I was still a little groggy but was excited to hear what she had to say.

She smiled and said calmingly and lovingly, "The pictures are completely clear."

I was overjoyed. Of course they were clear! God is constant and inherently good. I started praising the Lord and thanking Him for what He had done.

My mom told me that we would have to wait a couple of days for the biopsy results to confirm the eosinophil count, but the initial results indicated we were in the clear. That same weekend, we went to visit Faith Life Church to hear Pastor Gary Keesee.

His message was the start of a brand-new series talking about authority. After the sermon, I went up to Pastor Gary and asked him if he had time to come into agreement with me about what I believed. I quickly explained my lifelong battle with EoE, then told him how my faith had been transformed through what I had learned. I told him how I now believed God. That I was now healed and had no doubt in my mind that God had done this amazing thing.

He asked me what scripture I'd been standing on (trusting in) for that belief and I pointed out 1 Peter 2:24. Standing on scripture means you align your mind with the Word to renew your mind, becoming fully persuaded in what the Word says. You refuse anything the enemy bombards you with and believe in the words of the Bible.

Pastor Gary replied, "Good. God has already done it." He could tell I was still new in the Lord, a little timid and also hopeful, but I was also excited. He agreed with me and gave us some book recommendations to further and deepen my faith as well as some practical scriptural things to do, like stay in the Word.

The next morning, Sunday, we went back to Faith Life Church and sat in the front row. We heard the same message from Saturday night. In this second listening, we heard little bits we'd missed the first time.

When I went back home to South Georgia, my dad called me a few days later. "We got the results of the biopsy," he said. He let me know that my eosinophil count was still pretty high and not in the normal range. Any other time, I would have been deflated, sure that my EoE was still there. But this time, I rejected that thought.

And before I go on, please hear me. I'm not suggesting you ever ignore your doctor or your test results. You do not deny symptoms, sickness, or disease; you just deny it has the right to be in your body and in your life. You do not let it control you. Especially the pain of disease. You can choose to no longer put up with it.

I know that pain has an arguably loud voice, especially because I have experienced that firsthand and allowed it to affect me for so long. I want you to know that the blood of Jesus has a louder voice than any pain, sickness, disease, or bondage. He shut the mouth of the devil and everything the devil brought into this world and signed the contract with His blood, setting it in stone forever with His resurrection. That promise was what I clung to as I continued to be done with disease.

If you have been working to claim healing for yourself or to grow closer to God, do not think it's a coincidence when you're bombarded with thoughts of pain and worry. You may be constantly stressed, thinking of the chores you must do or the bills that need to be paid, and the load your illness has put on your life. I suggest always staying faithful and disciplined in your reading of the Word. Be resolute in the Lord because the war of pain is over.

I refused to let my test results be my focus. Every time those thoughts tried to creep in, I came back to Luke 10:19, which tells us that we have authority over all the power over the enemy.

I replied to my dad, "They won't stay that way."

After I hung up with him, I was driving home in my truck and said, "I command my body to line up with the Word of God. I command every cell in my body to work and function perfectly and properly just like they were created and designed to work and function, and I command any remnant of disease to flee my body in the name of Jesus!"

After that, I went back to my new life of faith and kept shopping for groceries and eating three or four meals a day. I still had no symptoms, no pain, and no discomfort when I ate. At every meal, I praised the Lord and thanked Him that this job was finished on the cross.

It was only after I firmly believed that Jesus' sacrifice was for my complete salvation, and that meant that I had complete and total health, that this transformation happened. I had to be absolutely and utterly convinced of this truth, and *then* proclaim my healing. I was able to hear the promises He had for me and know in my spirit that those promises manifested in my physical body.

For a year, I ate solid food and didn't use the inhalers or drink the formula. One morning in October of 2023, I was taking a shower and heard the Lord speak to me, "Go check your count."

I understood immediately that He wanted me to check my eosinophil count, which you can check through a blood test without the need for an endoscopy. A couple of days later, I couldn't shake the thought, so I arranged for a complete blood count test and went to the lab early one morning. After the nurse drew my blood, she mentioned I'd get the results within twenty-four hours.

The following morning, while I was at the gym with Jess, I received an email with the results. I logged in to review them, and as I scrolled through, all the indicators were in the green zone of normal.

Finally, at the bottom of the page, I saw the test said, "Eosinophils: normal."

I stood on the elliptical, just crying tears of joy and praising God. Jess started tearing up and praising the Lord with me. It was the most joyous feeling of thanksgiving for both of us and an absolute testament to the power of all I now knew about God's goodness.

I didn't say, "Thank God, now I know I'm healed!" I had already known that for quite some time. These blood test results were simply the Lord's way of confirming what I already knew, had been standing on, and believing in. Total and complete health. Deep down, I always wanted to see the results. Not because I had to see them in order to believe, but because seeing the evidence helps people to build hope and faith in their own journey. The Lord knew that and, in His righteous grace, showed me.

When I was a kid, I had such a challenging time sitting still in the church pews because the message I kept hearing made me feel like God was unjust. Over and over again, I heard pastors say that salvation was completed through Jesus' sacrifice. However, they didn't say the same about healing.

The Greek word for salvation is *sōtēria*.[3] One example of its use is in Romans 1:16 (NKJV), where the apostle Paul writes, "For I am not ashamed of the gospel of Christ, for it is the power of God to salvation for everyone who believes, for the Jew first and also for the Greek."

In the original Bible text, the word salvation used in that verse is the Greek word *sōtēria*, which by itself means, to rescue or deliver, safety, health and save. It is also derived from the root word *sōzō* which means: to deliver, preserve, heal or make whole.[4]

Over the course of time, many churches have watered down the meaning of salvation to simply the forgiveness of sins and eternal life. And yes, while that is definitely part of salvation, what some people forget is that your complete healing and total health are *also* part of that atonement.

If we are all saved through Jesus's sacrifice, then we are all also healed *by* His sacrifice. Over the years, I've heard so many people who said God specifically chose to heal them. I kept going to God, asking if he would simply *choose* me.

The idea that God chooses who to heal would make God unjust. Why would a loving Father choose to heal one person and yet, make another suffer a little longer for some reason only known to Him? That compromises His character of love and His Word in Romans 2:11 and in Acts 10:34, where it states that God shows no favoritism.

John 10:10 was that dividing line in the Bible for me, which provided me the proof of God's true character. "The thief comes only to steal, kill and destroy, I have come that they may have life, and have it more abundantly." (NIV)

3   "G4991 - sōtēria - Strong's Greek Lexicon (NKJV)." Blue Letter Bible. Web. 2024.
4   "G4982 - sōzō - Strong's Greek Lexicon (NKJV)." Blue Letter Bible. Web. 2024.

It's very simple—if there is something in your life that is stealing, killing, or destroying you—it is not from God. He wants us to live as fully and abundantly on earth as it is in Heaven. There's no sickness in Heaven, no disease, no lack, no depression, no addiction, because Jesus paid the price for us to live the abundant life of Heaven, here and now on earth. (Matthew 6:10)

The enemy, on the other hand, has spent his whole existence trying to impute the character of God because it's all he can do. The enemy has no power. The only power he has over believers is the power we give him, whether that may be through ignorance, lack of knowledge, or sin.

If you really want to align your thoughts with God, then look to the Word. There are many scriptures that emphasize meditating on scripture, or even just God in general. Romans 12:2 says you are transformed by the renewing of your mind.

I took that verse very seriously and gave everything I had in doing so because I wanted all of the old me and my old beliefs to be replaced with the truth of God's Word.

In another verse, Joshua 1:8, God speaks words of encouragement to Joshua. He guides him to meditate on the book of the law (the Word of God, AKA, the Bible), night and day. God tells Joshua that if he does this, then his way would be prosperous and he would have success. That's a direct promise from God to Joshua.

That's a promise to us, too.

I am so grateful that I did that because I now adore the Lord. When others look at me, I want them to see Jesus reflected in my actions, just like I saw in my mom back when I gave her such a hard time. Just like I've seen in my good friend, Chase, at work, and of course, just like I've seen in Jessica. I wanted to live a life full of God's love with all my loved ones and be the same inspiring example so many have been to me.

The way I approach everything in my life can be summed up in Colossians 3:22-25 (NASB 1995). "Slaves, in all things obey those who are your masters on earth, not with external service, as those who merely please men, but with sincerity of heart, fearing the Lord. Whatever you do, do your work heartily as for the Lord rather than for men, knowing that from the Lord you will receive the reward of the inheritance. It is the Lord Christ whom you serve. For he who does wrong will receive the consequences of the wrong which he has done, and that without partiality."

Jesus is telling us that, whatever we do and whomever we serve, our goal should not be to please the person or the situation in the worldly realm, but rather to serve them the same as we would serve Jesus.

As I've continued to ask God to exude Him in me in that way, I have slowly been able to feel less of me and more of Him. In chaotic situations, I often find myself not getting offended or aggravated, but instead responding with love and staying calm. That is what God wants from us and for us.

Stephanie

When Remington told me he was choosing to stand on the Word of God as he prepared for his endoscopy appointment in Ohio, I was amazed and so heartened because I could see the results of the prayers I had whispered for him. God promises us that seemingly impossible circumstances become possible through the power of prayer, and this moment (and many others) has been evidence of that.

Remington called me often before the appointment. We talked about the prayer time he'd been spending over his meals, plus some of the different types of foods that he'd enjoyed. He was firm in his belief that he was healed, and we were positive this endoscopy would be a success. At the end of the calls, he reminded me how great of a day it would be and how he could feel the goodness God wanted for him.

I was so thankful that my adult son could eat at the table with Jessica and start creating a strong foundation for a family of his own. The vision of Mike and I on the porch with our sons and grandchildren came back to me, and with Remington healthy and free of illness.

I could see him and his family eating at the holiday dinner table with us, building so many of the experiences and memories that the years of his disease had denied us. My heart nearly burst with joy when I thought about the future and the wonder of how his body had finally aligned with the promises of God.

When we realize how much power we have in those prayers and in the Lord, it is life changing. It's a true butterfly-like transformation when we know God gives us the power to heal, prosper, and bring Heaven to Earth.

On and off during our flight to Ohio, Rem and I recited verses amid our constant conversation. I waited for him to come to the recovery room after his endoscopy because I couldn't wait to tell him the initial scan appeared clear!

He smiled. "It doesn't matter what that scope shows, I know I'm healed."

I nodded with him in firm and solid agreement. I had seen and felt that in my own life and had no doubt God had worked the same amazing results in Rem's life.

Since we were in town, we went to Faith Life Church that Saturday evening to hear Gary Keesee at his Ohio church. At the end of the service, I watched in awe as Remington chose to walk to the front of the church and pray with Pastor Gary.

Pastor Gary listened to Rem's request and asked Rem, "What scripture are you standing on?"

That's such a powerful question, because most of us don't realize that we must stand on a bedrock of faith and on what God says in the Word, the written scripture. Otherwise, our plans and attempts to direct our lives quickly go awry. We must depend on God for that direction, and the entire GPS is right there in the Bible.

Rem responded with a verse we had mentioned several times on the plane ride: 1 Peter 2:24. I watched him pray with Pastor Gary and knew in my own heart that the years of fighting EoE were done for Remington. Finished. My son was healed! Glory to God!

This was such a powerful moment in both our lives. I clearly saw Remington healed in my soul and spirit, and I knew then that he was free from disease. God performs His Word!

When you are firm in your belief, you expect the best possible outcome because you know in every fiber of your being that God has got you. On that trip to Ohio, Rem went with expectancy of the promise of God, and I expected no other result but healing from God for Remington.

There is amazing power in our beliefs and declarations. There is wonder-working power in the belief that God is true to His promises to those who believe.

The next morning, we went back to Pastor Gary's church again. Even now, there is a special feeling that comes over me every time I step through the door. I know there is an anointing on this church's grounds. This time, we brought our entire Ohio family with us and sat in the front row to hear the same message again. It hit me just as profoundly the second time.

After the service, we also met with Pastor Drenda, and I shared with her how both her and Gary's teachings have transformed our lives. She prayed with us, and we hugged. I felt a connection with her as a mother and sister in Christ. Those bonds were so incredibly powerful in that moment. It felt as if the Holy Spirit flooded all of us with peace.

On the plane ride home, Rem kept saying, "I know I'm healed. I just know I'm healed. I don't care what the medical reports say or what the biopsy pictures show, I know that I am healed." It was as if he was reinforcing his own conviction.

We still didn't have the full results of the biopsy when Rem called us a couple days later. He was absolutely sobbing. It caught Mike and I off guard and for a second, and we worried.

Then he shared that he'd just had a moment that morning when the Holy Spirit came over him. In that moment, he had total clarity and *just knew* that he was healed. He said he couldn't describe the feeling but that he'd never felt anything like it before. Remington had dug into the Word of God and immersed himself into God's truths. The belief that was already in his spirit had manifested in his mind and he was fully persuaded.

After nineteen years of not eating the same foods the rest of us do, Rem is enjoying a new life and an abiding faith. For us, we had spent those years believing our son was allergic to all foods. Because we didn't know the truth of what God said about healing, we allowed the enemy, Satan, to steal nineteen years from our son's health.

None of that was done with ill intent. We were parents who worried, as any parent would, about the pain our child was suffering. We took the doctors' advice and did what we thought was right. At that time in his life, we were grateful for the medical treatment and nourishment he received.

Isaiah 54:17 (NKJV), "No weapon
formed against you shall prosper!"

This is, by far one of my favorite verses, and I quote it
multiple times a day, over everything that the Lord has blessed
me with including my family, home, and finances. It reminds
me where to put my focus when inevitable obstacles and
setbacks arise.

We need to be ready to deal with the challenges that
come our way, especially the tricky ones Satan throws at us.
Sometimes, we don't even get a moment to think about how
to solve our problems because they happen so suddenly. That's
why it's important to respond quickly, with scripture as our
reinforcement. That is what my sticky notes have reminded
me to do, time and time again.

At the end of this book, you'll find some
pocket scriptures so you can cut them out
and use them on your own tough days.

When it comes to our outlook regarding the problem, if the
first thing we say in a tough situation is something negative, it's
not a very good sign of the outcome. We unwittingly manifest
the negative result we don't want instead of empowering the
positive goodness God has for us.

Instead, begin with a prayer and reinforce it with some encouraging words from scripture, like the pieces of paper I carried in my pocket and referred to throughout the cancer diagnosis. This will help you bring Heaven on the scene and empower you through even the toughest of times.

There have been several demonstrations of speaking scripture and positive words through prayer to receive a desired outcome—which have turned into not just stronger faith for myself, but complete healing for those in my life!

One year, just before Christmas break, one of my students shared with me that his father had cirrhosis of the liver. He couldn't receive a liver transplant at the time because there were too many people ahead of him on the list, and the student said, "The doctors sent him home with hospice to die."

I knew this boy was in such distress, and feared losing his parent. I looked down and noticed he was wearing a WWJD (What Would Jesus Do?) bracelet, so I asked him if he was a believer and he said he was. I shared with him that I had been healed from cancer and that my son had also been healed.

I told him, "There is nothing that God can't do if we just believe."

I asked if I could pray for his dad and he agreed, so I put my hand on this young man's shoulder and commanded healing into his father's body, declaring that his father would live. We stood on 1 Peter 2:24 and I said the scripture aloud, calling it done in Jesus' name.

Afterwards, I told him about the "God Wants You Well" series that Remington and I had listened to; he texted his dad some links there on the spot because his father was also a believer.

We left for Christmas break two days later and were out of school for two weeks. Upon returning from break, this student couldn't wait to tell me that his dad had miraculously received a liver transplant and was sent home from the hospital, expecting a full recovery.

He hugged me and thanked me, and I said to him, "Remember this moment in your life when you saw the power of prayer work. Don't ever forget it. Jesus can do anything we believe He can do!"

This child saw his life transformed by prayer. It wasn't me; I was just the conduit for Jesus Christ!

Before I became more aware of the power in declaring scripture over my life, I know that what I often said while I was stressed made things even worse. The more I focused on the problem, the more it affected me.

Satan constantly tries to trick us this way, to get us to dwell in the negative and bring us down with lies and temptations. When you read John 10:10, it spells that out by telling us that Jesus came so we can have a full and good life, unlike the thief (Satan) who only wants to kill and destroy.

Hosea 4:6 also talks about how we suffer because of our own lack of knowledge. This is especially true for a lack of knowledge in how to tap into the Kingdom of God. We don't know *how* to ask for help from above, and this makes us more vulnerable to the negativity of the enemy.

That's why, for me, these Kingdom principles are so vitally important to grasp and take to heart. But it was only through much trial and error that I tapped into these laws of the Kingdom about prayer. Once I did, I began seeing those prayers answered. When that change happened in me, my prayers went from "what-if" to "Yes, and Amen."

If you stop to think about how prayer works, it's not a dictum from God, and it's not a constant plea. It's a two-way communication with the Father. We aren't just talking to Him, we are also taking the time to *listen*. Listening is just as important as talking, sometimes even more so because, in those interactions, we're more open to seeing the power of our faith. The Lord constantly plants seeds of faith and suggestions of scripture into your spirit to guide you.

Many people have asked me, "Well, how do you know if God is talking to you?"

My answer is simple. "How do you know God *isn't* talking to you? To hear Him, you have to sit quietly and take the time to listen. Open your heart, your mind, and your ears."

In John 10:27 (NKJV), Jesus said, "My sheep hear My voice..."

We are all so busy, buzzing around our schedules and to-dos, that we fail to see the bigger picture—that God is there, just waiting for us to request His guidance through prayer. If we get quiet enough, we can hear His voice in our ear. Now, this happens to me often.

One day, I felt the nudge to talk to a young woman with her dog outside of our grocery store. I was in a hurry and really wanted to get back to my car and on to the next to-do, but instead I listened to that inner voice and went over to her. I asked if I could help her in any way, which started with filling the dog's water bowl, and began a deep and emotional conversation about her struggles and the loss of her sister. I then asked if I could pray with her.

She had fallen on hard times and was concerned that she was dirty and unclean, and didn't want to be a bother. I told her that didn't matter. I simply saw her as another of God's children and told her she was beautiful, as Jesus would see her. I spoke blessings over her life and reassured her of God's undying love for her.

This was a woman with a massive mountain in her life that had left her feeling defeated and lost, maybe even ashamed. Those ten minutes I spent with her reminded her of who she was in Christ, and she had the power to move that mountain. I never saw her again, but I am confident that, because I responded to that nudge from God, those minutes gave her exactly what she needed that day.

Many of us will sit and wait on hold with a credit card company for longer than it takes to spend some time with God, or we will ignore the voice telling us to stop and pray with someone in need. Instead of spending thirty minutes waiting for someone to answer the phone or focusing on your massive list of tasks, why not spend that little bit of time reading the Word and talking to Him? Why not take the time to stop for another in need?

If you set aside time for the Lord in prayer and read His Word, you will be so amazed at how you will begin to see things differently. The more time you spend in God's presence, the more you begin to see things from His perspective. You'll begin to see people and situations through His eyes. His perspective is truth, and every moment you spend in that truth brings you closer to Him, and Him closer to you.

James 4:7-8 (ESV), "Submit yourselves therefore to God. Resist the devil, and he will flee from you. Draw near to God, and he will draw near to you."

That is our hope for you in writing this book. We hope that you come to a point where you declare sickness and disease gone from your life. That you can tap into this promise of healing and walk in total health. That you can speak to the mountain in your life and it will move, as God has promised. It moved for our family, for Remington, and it will move for you. All in Glory to God!

Chapter 7

The Principle of Unity

Stephanie and Remington

When we began our journey to write this book, we had no idea how much it would bring us closer together and inspire so many incredible conversations, both with each other and with others. We are so grateful to Jesus for this opportunity to share it with you.

You are part of our journey, too, and when we say "we" here, we are including every single person who is seeking truth, enlightenment, fellowship, and hope. Our "we" is anyone who wants to know more about our amazing Lord, Jesus Christ.

The truths we've learned over the past several years have transformed our understanding of God and His Kingdom. We now know that the Lord's intention is that we walk in full health, so it's our job to align with God's Word to receive this promise.

Our family has done this by studying scripture determinedly and declaring this written truth over our lives through prayer, both in our own faith journeys and when we come together in fellowship. We pray in belief of the outcomes of God's goodness that comes to us because of Christ's sacrifice on the cross for all of us. We pray that the outcomes, like financial stability and full health, have already come to us and are here to stay.

When we study, we rely on scripture as our source of knowledge and guidance because this is God's way of teaching us. It's His way of training our hearts and minds to defend against any negative thought, proverbial mountain, or physical obstacle that comes our way. This is also to fortify our belief and add more to our toolbox in fighting the attacks of the enemy (Satan).

---

2 Timothy 3:16 (NIV), "All Scripture is God-breathed and is useful for teaching, rebuking, correcting and training in righteousness."

That's why these truths are so important to us and why we want to leave them with you. They have provided us with a new perspective and an armor of truth. We see ourselves and our circumstances in such a light that we no longer live in those what-if moments of fear or frustration when hard times come. We no longer worry that our prayers are unheard. We thank God for the blessings He has already given us and that our burdens be cast down and rebuked.

The way we have received healing is also not the only way. This is just the path God has shown us and led our family to.

God is not limited to a certain "box" of healing; He will meet you where you are and He knows just what you need.

For my mother, it was understanding God's truth and the power of spoken words, and for me (Rem), it was being fully persuaded and trusting in His promise above everything else. This journey may look very different for you, but the foundation of Jesus' finished work on the cross remains the same.

That is especially true when it comes to medical needs and decisions, which are a personal choice that should be made based on information and faith—not out of fear—and always with proper council.

God will work within any situation if it means His child is made whole. This includes whether you're deciding to take medication or undergo an operation. Follow the doctor's plan, but also seek God's wisdom and He will direct your steps.

For someone who is struggling with a mountain in their life: You can go to Jesus. He is the way maker and is standing there with open arms. For anyone who has grown apart from their faith: He will still hear you. He's not mad at you, He loves you.

If it's healing you need, research scriptures that speak of healing. If it's finances you need or guidance, then research those scriptures too. Begin by setting time aside for God or by reading a passage from the Bible. If you don't know where to start, check out our suggestions for praying at the end of this book. He will come to you when you seek Him and transform your life beyond what you can even think up. God wants you well.

For us, strengthening our faith in those times of need required (and still does!) turning to scripture when the desired outcome was not yet visible in our lives. We struggled for so long in diagnosing and treating diseases that came upon our family, and some days it became difficult to muster that faith. Yet together, and only with God, we prevailed. We never gave up hope in the outcome once we learned that it was available for us, just as it is for you. This is available to all!

The beautiful news is that when we turn to God in need, confident in His promise to provide for us, He will. Even if this doesn't come as we expect it, our trust is rooted in His Word, which assures us, "Ask and you shall receive." (Matthew 7:7) (Mark 11:24)

Sometimes, prayers are as simple as praying over our meals, which have a different meaning in light of what our family has gone through. We thank the Lord that His blessings cover our food and drink, and then we command what we want the food to do for our bodies, which is to nourish, strengthen, and energize.

Your prayers do not have to be long and drawn out. You can keep it simple. (This is an example of how I, Rem, pray over my meals.)

"Father, thank you for this food, I command it to nourish my body in Jesus' name. Amen."

Simple, but done in faith.

Church together also looks very different. We're able to feel at peace in the pews while we grab hold of the messages of God's Word. The sermons at Faith Life Church are some of the most insightful for us, and Saturday's weekly online service is often a can't-miss.

Many of these sermons resonate with us because they discuss the truths contained in God's Word, and they are backed by scripture and testimonies of people who have experienced freedom, just like 2 Timothy 3:16 states.

Scripture is our tool, here for us to pick up and build a strong house of faith, belief, and for the Holy Spirit to teach us, perfect us, and settle us through the scripture.

So, why not speak with God about your life and the lives of your family? Use God's Word as a protective shield when you pray and place a hedge of protection around you, your family, home, vehicles, finances, pets, decisions, etc....

And to also build the image of what He says about who you are on the inside:

─────────────────

I am beautiful and strong "because I am fearfully and wonderfully made." (Psalm 139:14)

─────────────────

─────────────────

I live in peace because You have "not given us a spirit of fear, but of power, love and a sound mind." (2 Timothy 1:7)

─────────────────

This will renew your confidence in God's plan that we are to walk in heaven on earth.

━━━━━━━━━━

2 Peter 1:3-4 (NIV), "His divine power has given us everything we need for a godly life through our knowledge of Him who called us by His own glory and goodness. Through these He has given us His very great and precious promises, so that through them you may participate in the divine nature, having escaped the corruption in the world caused by evil desires."

━━━━━━━━━━

The message of the Bible holds this truth. It tells us of God's extraordinary act of love—sending Jesus (God Almighty) from Heaven, embodying human flesh, and enduring immense suffering on the cross—so brutal that His body was unrecognizable. This was the ultimate sacrifice, taking the full punishment of sin, setting you free, justifying and acquitting you forever of your transgressions.

God does give us free will to choose Him, and if you find yourself reflecting on your faith, maybe unsure if you've truly committed to Him or you're wishing to reaffirm your decision, know that God is listening and that you can go to Him.

You can be sure today. You can say this prayer out loud and set in stone your eternal destination and receive Jesus as your Savior:

Father, thank You for sending Jesus to take the punishment for my sin. I repent for the way I've lived apart from You, and now I invite You, Jesus, to come into my life to guide me and to be my Lord and Savior. Cleanse me of unrighteousness and show me the workings of Your Kingdom. I believe that You died and rose again and that, from this day forward, my name is written in the Lamb's book of life. I pray this in Jesus' name. Amen.

God's promises are real. They're for you.

As we continue to grow deeper in our relationship with God, we will also continue to be here for you. We look forward to hearing about the power of God operating in your life, and seeing you grasp your identity in Christ.

You were fearfully and wonderfully made in God's divine image, designed for a specific purpose with specific gifts, talents, and abilities that no one else on Earth has. You don't have to settle for anything less than the fullness of what Jesus purchased for you on the cross.

Remember: You are never alone, and we're all here to unite as children of God, in both health and happiness.

A word from Remington

I am so thankful for how close God has pulled me to Him these past several years. I want you to know that the stories in the Bible are not just stories, the Bible is not just a book, and Jesus is not a fairytale. This is very real. Words cannot explain my gratitude that, even when I forsook Him and didn't pursue Him, He pursued me. And He is pursuing you.

John 3:16 isn't just a verse, it's a demonstration of God's heart and love toward us, His precious creation. Sin had to be dealt with. God Almighty left Heaven and, being limited to flesh, took it on and entered this fallen, broken world to bear the penalty of sin so that we don't have to.

This has forever changed my life and led to a full restoration from what I once feared was a life-plaguing illness to eating freely, being able to grow closer to the Lord, and continue to experience God's love on deeper levels.

This change in me, of coming to Him, is the same change God hopes for all of us, and I sincerely hope for you as well. (2 Peter 3:9)

The Principle of Faith

An Example of How to Pray

Stephanie

Many of us may struggle with exactly how to pray. Throughout most of my life, I prayed to God for guidance and answers for myself. Then, as I got older, for my friends and family.

However, when I prayed out of desperation for God to show me what to do in those darker moments, I felt stuck. I felt abandoned by the end of my pleading because I thought my prayers were going unanswered. I worried that I wasn't praying "right" or that my prayers weren't as effective as they could be. Eventually, I thought that maybe it wasn't God's will for these things to come to pass in my life as I'd hoped. This left me feeling frustrated while I struggled to connect with God in my prayer life.

What I didn't know was that both the power of prayer and the authority I have in Christ would be revealed to me in the pages of the Bible. The deeper I got into the Word, the more I realized that the answers I sought were already there! These scriptures held everything I needed to experience health, prosperity, and eternal life, and they have guided my prayers ever since.

To help you get started, I wrote this as a template so you can begin to draw closer to God and tap into these Kingdom principles. This is not an absolute formula on how to pray, but more of a guide. It's up to you to research the scriptures and find the ones that relate to your need. Finding those verses is a key piece to this and will allow you to personalize your prayers to your situation.

Matthew 6:9-13 is a good place to start as it's a model of how we're to pray. We're to pray to the Father in the name of Jesus and the following scriptures are a reference for this: Luke 11:9-10; John 14:13-14; John 15:16; John 16:23; John 16:26; Colossians 3:17; James 4:3; 1 John 3:21-22; and 1 John 5:14-15.

It's important to know what scripture we're referring to and standing on when we pray, because God's Word is His will—and His Word is alive. It is how we reinforce our prayers.

Prayer is our communication channel, our walkie-talkie if you will, that allows us to develop a relationship with God and strengthen our faith in His promises; and every prayer begins with faith. This is the substance that fortifies and empowers our words. It's the confidence and belief needed to back them up. The Bible tells us that faith as small as a mustard seed can blossom our prayers into divine manifestations, and this is how God's promises come to fruition in our lives.

While talking to God, prayer also involves listening to Him for guidance and direction. James 1:5 (NIV) says, "If any of you lacks wisdom, he should ask God, who gives generously to all without finding fault, and it will be given to you."

This verse tells us directly that we are to pray and ask God for the knowledge we're seeking and that it will be generously received when we do. When we regularly do this and spend time with God in prayer, we build a sense of closeness with Him as we receive His wisdom. We build the assurance that He is listening to our prayers, and we *know* He hears us! James 4:8 (NKJV) tells us, "Draw near to God and He will draw near to you."

Mark 11:24 (NIV) also states, "Therefore I tell you, whatever you ask for in prayer, believe that you have received it, and it will be yours."

1 John 5:14-15 (NIV) reiterates this even further, "This is the confidence we have in approaching God: that if we ask anything according to His will, He hears us. And if we know that He hears us—whatever we ask—we know that we have what we asked of Him."

When you pray, fully believe that you will receive.

This is one of the guiding tenets of prayer that will bring you closer to God and His goodness for your life. It's about believing in your heart that your prayer is answered the very minute you pray, even if the thing you are praying for hasn't happened—yet. You stay in that state of mind of total belief in the outcome, and praise Jesus that it is done.

To help that belief sink in even further, I refer to scripture that aligns with my prayers so I continually reinforce the message of God's promises. My favorite way of doing this is by carrying a small written scripture in my pocket so it's easy to access and right there for me to pull out. This is how I stand in His Word, choosing to speak in thanks with confidence, like this:

Paraphrasing Proverbs 8:35. (AMP): "Thank you, that I have wisdom, favor and grace from You, Lord."

Having faith when we pray, even as small as a mustard seed, is a Kingdom principle. It-will bring you closer to God and His goodness for your life. When you have faith that the outcome is already complete, you are in alignment with God's Word.

Prayers for Healing

When you need healing, reach out to Jesus! The Bible tells us that, as believers, we have the power of the Holy Spirit living on the inside of us, the same power Christ had when He walked on Earth. The Bible also tells us that Jesus took our sicknesses so we could be made whole, set free from sin and disease.

We see this in Isaiah 53:5, where the Word says that Jesus took our infirmities, sorrows, transgressions, and iniquities and that it was all placed upon Him on the cross. When we believe the infirmities of sickness are no longer ours to bear, our prayers can begin to command the body to line up with the Word of God.

The Bible also says that Jesus healed all. Matthew 4:23 (NIV) states, "Jesus went throughout Galilee, teaching in their synagogues, proclaiming the good news of the Kingdom, and healing every disease and sickness among the people."

Notice the words *Kingdom* and *every*. If you have accepted Jesus Christ as your Savior, as a believer, you are a part of God's Kingdom. Jesus was already a part of the Kingdom because He was God in the flesh, and now, we have access to the Kingdom because we are His children. (Romans 8:16-17)

The word *every* in this verse refers to disease, just as I mentioned before. There was nothing that Jesus could not heal. No disease nor sickness was (or is) off limits. Allow those words to sink in and feed your spirit. Remember: God does not lie. This is Truth. Believe it! (Hebrews 6:18)

Another part of that truth is written plainly in Luke 10:19 (NIV), when Jesus says, "I have given you authority to trample on snakes and scorpions and to overcome all the power of the enemy, nothing will harm you."

This is the case the moment we accept Jesus into our hearts as believers. In Acts 1:8 (NKJV), Jesus also says: "But you shall receive power when the Holy Spirit has come upon you; and you shall be witnesses to Me in Jerusalem, and in all Judea and Samaria, and to the ends of the earth."

We have this power through the Holy Spirit to claim what Jesus' sacrifice provided us. That's what makes believers different than nonbelievers. We have His authority to overcome the evil of this world, and sickness is one of those evils. Declare it gone with a prayer for healing.

With these prayers, we are bringing Heaven on the scene. We are speaking God's Word over our bodies, our lives, our finances, and our difficulties. God's Word is power and life! God's Word transforms! His Word transformed my life and Remington's life, and His Word can transform yours.

A personalized prayer for healing, spoken with confidence and authority, might look like this (and a note: the Bible verses are for reference as I pray, the rest of the prayer is a personalized declaration):

"Father, Your Word says it is Your will that I be healed. Therefore, in the name of Jesus, I command that my body be in line with the Word of God. I command all cells to return to normal. I command (*the named disease, calamity, or distress*) to leave my body *now*.

I stand on 1 Peter 2:24 that says, By His stripes I am healed. I stand on Jeremiah 30:17 that says, God restores health to my body and heals wounds.

I'm declaring this now over my body. So, body, line up with what the Word of God says. God's Word does not return void, and these words *will* accomplish what I desire and achieve the purpose for which I sent it, according to Isaiah 55:11.

This tells us that Your Word produces results, Lord; these words produce healing.

Thank you, Jesus! Amen."

After speaking this command over your body and taking authority over the illness, you stand on the Word of God and believe it done! This can be difficult when the devil attempts to entertain you with thoughts of fear, doubt, or despair, but don't allow that emotion to take over.

Fight back with God's Word. Guard your mouth and your heart from speaking words of defeat. Speak Words of life! Luke 6:45 (NIV) says, "The mouth speaks what the heart is full of," so we must be careful of what we're speaking aloud and ultimately, over our life.

Remember Job, who lost everything by speaking of his fears? You must stay in agreement with what the Word of God says. Reach for the Bible and quote scripture when those thoughts arise, especially when it comes to your health.

I'm not saying to ignore your doctor's knowledge if you have a medical issue; in fact, heed it. The Lord gave mankind the wisdom to discover medicine and we may need the doctor's wisdom about a medical situation we're experiencing.

Maybe medical treatment is suggested, or medicine is prescribed to help regulate the body or to cure infection. Sometimes, the body needs a little help, and doctors can be used by God to help us.

Throughout it all, simply pray. When you take a medication, thank the Lord that it will fight off the infection. God is the Chief Physician. Speak life, love, and abundance over your body through prayer and as you do, it will reward you with more life, love, and abundance, through the power of God's Word.

A personalized prayer to defeat life's storms that roll in might look like this:

> "Father, thank You for my blessings. While these circumstances are difficult now and I believe they shall soon pass, show me that I am strong and courageous.
>
> I am not afraid; I am not discouraged, for You, Lord, are with me wherever I go.
>
> I stand on 2 Timothy 1:7 that says, For God does not give me a spirit of fear, but of power, love, and of sound mind.
>
> In Jesus' name. Amen."

I use these scriptures as the basis for a Declaration I speak aloud, as if it has already been done, to reinforce what God has already promised. I provided a sample Declaration, too, to get you started writing or speaking your own. A declaration of this prayer might look like this:

"Thank you, Jesus, that I have power, love and a sound mind."

It can be tempting to doubt when you are tired or frustrated, but no matter what, don't speak words that go against your prayer. The Word of God acts as our defense against the enemy's attacks. Attacks like disease and destruction. Hebrews 4:12 (NIV) says, "For the word of God is alive and active. Sharper than any doubled-edged sword."

Though you may not feel that you're healthy now, keep quoting scripture over your body that reinforces God's promises. Use the Word of God as your weapon! It might take time for your body to get into alignment, as it did for me, but keep believing in the powerful life source of God's Word.

The more you keep speaking the Word of God over your life and the more you are in the Word, the more you come into agreement and belief. Faith will rise in your heart that God will do as He has promised.

The good news is that you will get to a point where nothing 'sticks' to you or clouds your vision in what God promises. You'll begin to see yourself well and walking in health because of what His Word says.

Prayers of Petition

When it comes to praying for yourself or others in your life who have a need or are seeking a desired outcome, I wanted to give you an example of a prayer of petition. A prayer of petition is asking God to do something. We can reach out and declare that these things are already done in our lives when we pray to God through petitions.

For example, if you're in need of a scholarship, that would be a desire that you have, so it's a petition. If you are in need of wisdom on making a decision regarding medical treatment, that would also be a petition. When we pray for someone who says they need God's direction for their lives and are ready in their heart to receive it, that would also be a petition.

I have certainly experienced the power of petitions in my own life, particularly as it relates to Remington. Once I prayed for Rem's heart to be softened and for him to embrace the teachings I was learning, I simply believed that it was done. I didn't say anything that contradicted those prayers but believed it had already happened the moment my prayers were spoken aloud.

I'd say something like, "Thank you Jesus, that Rem's heart is softened to embrace Your Word over his life. Thank you that Mark 11:23-24 is my reminder that You will move this mountain and that Your Word is true. Thank you, Jesus!"

Petitions are when we ask, believe, and receive. However, petitions should be aligned with God's Kingdom principles, meaning, we should pray according to scripture. We shouldn't speak a prayer and ask God for something bad to happen to someone else. We're not praying for someone to break a leg so we can win the race. This would go against what God says—which is that we are to love others as we love ourselves.

Mike and I experienced the power of petitions, firsthand (which we learned from Gary and Drenda Keesee's teachings), when we were looking for some land. I had recently learned about the principle of sowing seeds at a church which aligned with the Biblical principles of God's Kingdom. We trusted that God would multiply our offering and shine favor and blessings on us when making this purchase. We donated and wrote on the check: "40-60 acres in Georgia or Tennessee for $60-70k."

Placing our hands on the rectangular slip, we prayed and stood on scripture, affirming our manifestation. Another sticky note on our refrigerator read, "Thank you, Jesus, for this land," a daily reminder infused with faith. We envisioned the property, believing it was enroute to us. One night, I even dreamt of a young girl playing on that open land, a vision I shared with Mike, affirming our ownership of the forthcoming property.

Weeks later, an acquaintance connected us with someone in Georgia selling forty-one acres for $70,000. The land had been partially cleared, and I had wanted a property with trees. When we went there for the inspection, we were delighted to see that the hardwood trees remained intact, scattered across the property.

After some negotiation, we secured the forty-one acres for $60,000, allowing us just enough funds for cleaning up the area. This purchase not only granted us the land, but also led Mike to a men's group at a local church, introducing us to remarkable individuals.

By sowing a seed, maintaining faith, and praying with a belief that land was on its way to us, we witnessed divine orchestration. That land seemed financially unattainable by worldly standards, but God's provision tailored it perfectly to align with our budget. Praise the Lord!

Here is an example of my personalized prayer when I needed wisdom for our situation:

> "Lord, thank you for all that You are! We come to You Father, in Jesus' name for the (*need/change/ petition*) that I am asking for. (*State the exact need/ change/petition*). I stand on Psalm 84:11 that says, You are a sun and shield, You bestow favor and honor and withhold no good thing from those whose walk is blameless. Amen!"

By being strategic with our prayers and using scripture as our weapon and shield, we can declare these blessings that God promises.

I've witnessed firsthand what happens when people speak scripture over their lives and believe in the powerful name of Jesus. Lives are completely transformed!

The Lord will meet us wherever we are in our faith journey and prayer life. As believers, we must do our part and become active in our faith to receive God's promises. When you do, watch what happens next as the supernatural power of God overflows into your life!

Pocket Scriptures

To keep the Word close to your heart, we've listed several powerful scriptures that our family stands on for comfort and guidance. These verses are for you to carry wherever you go. Feel free to cut them out, put them in your pocket, or share them with a friend. Speak these words aloud as a declaration of God's promises over your life when you are in a time of need. Some of these scriptures are already personalized so that you can declare your specific need. To tailor these even more, replace You/We with I when you say them out loud.

I like to also like to use these scriptures as the basis for a Declaration I speak aloud, as if it has already been done, to reinforce what God has already promised. I provided a sample Declaration, too, to get you started on writing or speaking your own.

For example:

> **1 Peter 2:24 NKJV** – "He himself bore our sins" in his body on the cross, so that we might die to sins and live for righteousness; "by his wounds you have been healed."

> **Declaration:** Jesus bore my sins in His body on the cross, so that I might die to sin and live for righteousness, by His wounds I have been healed.

Below are scriptures from the NIV version of the Bible. Maybe you have a need for...

HEALING

1. **Isaiah 53:5** – "But he was pierced for our transgressions, he was crushed for our inequities; the punishment that brought us peace was upon him, and by his wounds we are healed."

2. **Jeremiah 30:17** – "But I will restore you to health and heal your wounds, declares the Lord."

3. **Psalm 107:20** – "He sent forth His word and healed them; he rescued them from the grave."

4. **Proverbs 4:20-22** – "My son, pay attention to what I say; listen closely to my words. Do not let them out of your sight, keep them within your heart; for they are life to those who find them, and health to a man's whole body."

5. **Nahum 1:9** – "Whatever they plot against the Lord, he will bring to an end; trouble will not come a second time."

6. **Psalm 103:2-3** – "Praise the Lord, O my Soul, and forget not all His benefits – who forgives all your sins and heals all your diseases."

PRAISE

7. **Psalm 47:2** – "How awesome is the Lord Most High, the great King over all the earth!"

BATTLE FEAR

8. **2 Timothy 1:7** – "For God did not give us a spirit of timidity, but a spirit of power, of love, and of self-discipline."

9. **Joshua 1:9** – "Have I not commanded you? Be strong and courageous. Do not be terrified; do not be discouraged; for the LORD your God will be with you wherever you go."

WISDOM

10. **Psalm 19:7** – "The law of the LORD is perfect, reviving the soul. The statutes of the LORD are trustworthy, making wise the simple."

11. **Proverbs 3:5-6** – "Trust in the Lord with all your heart and lean not on your own understanding; in all your ways acknowledge him, and he will make your paths straight."

FAVOR

12. **Psalm 5:12** – "For surely, O Lord, you bless the righteous; you surround them with your favor as with a shield."

13. **2 Corinthians 5:17** – "Therefore, if anyone is in Christ, he is a new creation; the old has gone, the new has come!"

SALVATION

14. **John 3:16** – "For God so loved the world that he gave his one and only Son, that whoever believes in him shall not perish but have eternal life."

PROSPERITY

15. **Deuteronomy 1:11** – "May the LORD, the God of your fathers, increase you a thousand times and bless you as He has promised!"

16. **Philippians 4:19** – "And my God will meet all your needs according to his glorious riches in Christ Jesus."

About the Authors

Stephanie Walls

Stephanie and her husband, Mike, have two sons, Dalton, and Remington. She has taught English for over twenty-two years and her friends like to call her "Miss Sunshine," due to her positive and bubbly demeanor. She's dedicated to helping others and spreading joy in her community, and hosts a weekly bible study in her home. Family and faith are her driving forces in life, and she is a firm believer that, with God, anything is possible.

Remington Walls

Remington is a Valdosta State University graduate living in South Georgia with his wife, Jessica, and their dog and two cats. Though Remington faced an impossible situation, he believes it is the outlook that determines the outcome. He is a persistently driven young man with a love to share Jesus with everyone he meets. An avid lover of the outdoors, engaging in sports with friends and playing frisbee with his dog are some of his favorite pastimes.